ADVANCED**BLUES** **GUITAR**SOLOING

Move Beyond Pentatonics to Solo with Advanced Scales, Arpeggios & Substitutions

SHAUN**BAXTER**

FUNDAMENTAL**CHANGES**

Advanced Blues Guitar Soloing

Move Beyond Pentatonics to Solo with Advanced Scales, Arpeggios & Substitutions

ISBN: 978-1-78933-471-5

Published by **www.fundamental-changes.com**

Copyright © 2025 Shaun Baxter

Edited by Tim Pettingale

For over 350 free guitar lessons with videos check out:

www.fundamental-changes.com

Join our free Facebook Community of Cool Musicians

www.facebook.com/groups/fundamentalguitar

Tag us for a share on Instagram: **FundamentalChanges**

Cover Image Copyright: Shaun Baxter

Blues Solos #1, #2, #3 and #4 performed by Shaun Baxter,
recorded and mixed at W.M. Studios by Phil Hilborne
All other audio, performed recorded and mixed at Brakenhurst Studios by Shaun Baxter

All transcriptions by Shaun Baxter

Contents

About the Author

Shaun Baxter is a world-renowned guitar player and the UK's most experienced and respected rock guitar teacher.

He was a founder member of The Guitar Institute in London in 1986 (which was partnered with the London College of Music and became the biggest trade school for guitar in Europe), where he taught every week for over twenty years. He went on to be Head of Guitar at Guitar-X in London before, in 2003, becoming an owner and the Academic Director of The Academy of Music and Sound (AMS), a national network of musical schools, opening centres in Exeter, Southampton, Swindon, Aylesbury, Hitchin, Gateshead, Birmingham, Edinburgh and Glasgow. At one point, via their various apprenticeship schemes, AMS were the biggest employer in the Scottish music industry and whose alumni includes Lewis Capaldi.

Shaun composed the world's first Grade 8 Guitar syllabus for Trinity College, wrote the UK's National Operational Standards (NOS) for music performance, and contributed to magazines such as *The Guitar Magazine*, *Guitar World*, *Metal Hammer* and *Guitar Techniques* (for whom he wrote a popular and influential column every month for 27 years).

Through his teaching, Shaun helped to pioneer popular music education in the UK and taught many prominent guitar players and teachers, such as Rick Graham, Andy James, Jon Gomm and Justin Sandercoe, as well as many others who have found fame in the music industry with artists such as Public Image Ltd, Asia, Craig David, Moby, Wynton Marsalis, Haken, Martin Taylor, Steve Hackett, Rick Wakeman, Mike Oldfield, The Art of Noise, Leo Sayer, Pet Shop Boys, Roger Waters and Queen.

During the '90s, Shaun was a member of the Composition Department at the London College of Music and also lectured at Brunel University, Leeds College of Music, University of West London, Bath Spa University, Coventry University and Rostock University of Music and Drama (East Germany).

In 1993 Shaun recorded his ground-breaking *Jazz Metal* solo album. He has performed with players such as Uli Jon Roth (Scorpions), Neil Murray (Whitesnake, Black Sabbath) and Ron "Bumblefoot" Thal (Guns & Roses), and also toured the world and/or recorded with artists such as Princess, John Sloman (Gary Moore/ Uriah Heep), Todd Rundgren and Carl Palmer of Emerson Lake and Palmer.

> "He is one of the greatest musicians I have played with."
> – Carl Palmer, legendary progressive rock drummer

As an artist, Shaun has been an official endorsee of Marshall Amplification, Cornford Amplification, Fender Guitars, Patrick Eggle Guitars, Line 6 effects, Two-Note Audio Engineering, and Picato Strings.

Finally, Shaun was one of only 8 heavy metal guitar players (along with Edward Van Halen, Joe Satriani, Steve Vai, Yngwie Malmsteen, Nuno Bettencourt, Michael Schenker and Paul Gilbert) featured in the world's biggest-selling music book, *Guitar: A Complete Guide for the Player* (2002).

He appeared in a list of "The top 50 rock guitar players since the 1980s" in an article which appeared in *Guitarist* magazine, and was also included in *The Guitarist Book of Guitar Players* (1994), which details "the world's most influential guitarists and bass players", in which *Jazz Metal* topped its 50 recommended fusion guitar recordings.

Shaun is the bestselling author of

Chromatic Lead Guitar Techniques

Dominant Pentatonic Scale Guitar Soloing

Creative Intervallic Guitar Soloing

Legato and Tapping Rock Guitar Etudes.

Learn more at www.Fundamental-Changes.com

Introduction

This book is aimed at intermediate to advanced players who are confident with pentatonic-based blues playing but want to expand their vocabulary.

Rather than focusing on playing over sophisticated chord changes in a blues context, we will explore ways to imply more complex tonalities over the most basic twelve-bar blues progression: I – IV – V.

A7 (I)			
1	2	3	4

D7 (IV)		A7 (I)	
5	6	7	8

E7 (V)	D7 (IV)	A7 (I)	E7 (V)
9	10	11	12

As a vehicle, we will use the same backing track throughout the book. It features a shuffle feel (a triplet-based rhythm) similar to songs like *Hideaway* and *The Wanderer*.

The musical examples are written in 12/8. This is a standard way of notating triplet-based rhythms without having to write a "3" over every group, as would be necessary in 4/4. If that seems unclear, don't worry. Simply follow the tab, listen to the recorded examples, and trust your ears.

Please make use of the audio files provided. To fully understand the material, it's essential to hear it in context. In fact, I recommend starting by listening to the final four solos before reading the book in detail. This will give you a clear idea of how the concepts sound when applied musically.

Although we will begin by outlining the most basic approaches to blues playing, the examples in this book focus on implying harmony over the existing chord changes. That is, suggesting chords and progressions in our solos that are not explicitly written into the basic score.

By studying the ideas presented here, you will learn to approach the blues as a progression with distinct sections, each supporting a specific type of musical vocabulary.

Three Basic Soloing Approaches

Although we will spend most of this book exploring ways to imply more sophisticated harmony, it's important to begin by acknowledging the three most common soloing approaches.

Use The A Minor Blues Scale Over the Entire Progression

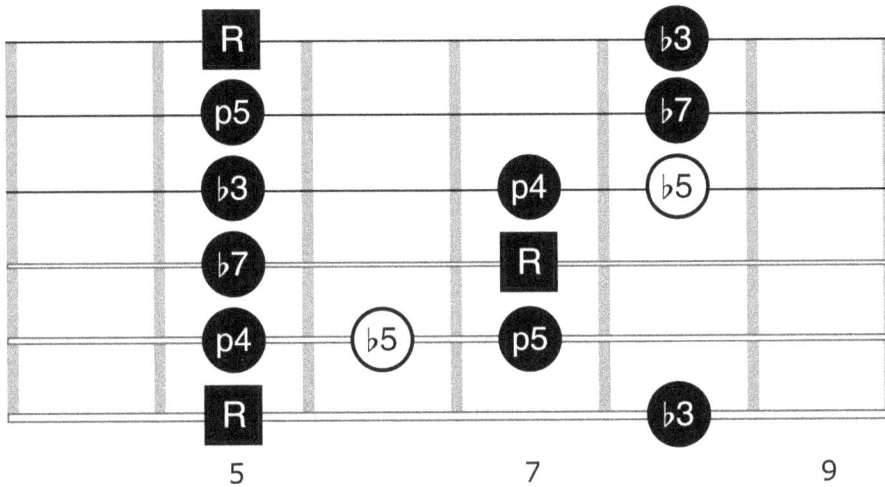

Use A Mixolydian in Conjunction with the A Minor Blues Scale Over A7, and Return to A Minor Blues Over D7 and E7

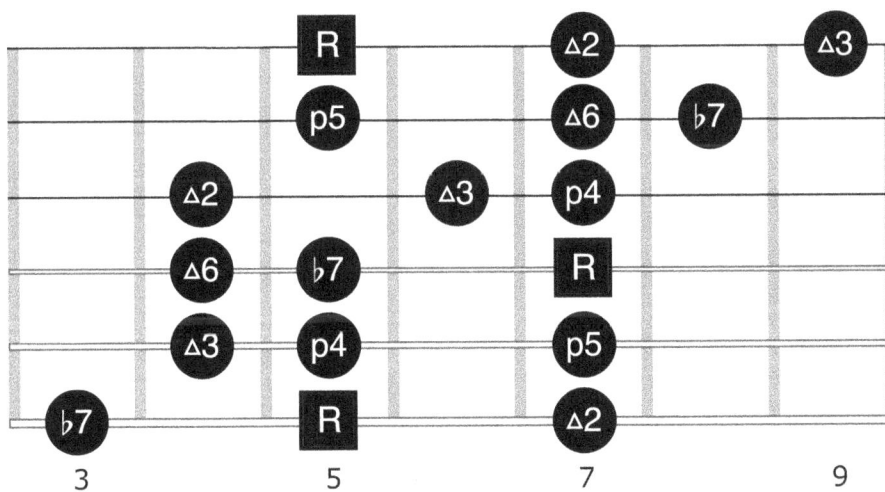

Use Mixolydian from the Root of Each Dominant Chord

With this final approach, it's especially important to focus on targeting chord tones (the root, 3rd, 5th and b7 of each chord). Doing so allows you to outline the underlying harmony and help the listener hear the movement of the progression.

Mixolydian Blues Hybrid Scale

Due to the natural blend between Mixolydian and the minor blues scale, many players prefer to think in terms of a nine-note hybrid scale. This scale combines Mixolydian with added tension tones (the b3 and b5), providing a colourful palette for phrasing.

A Mixolydian Blues Hybrid	A	B	B#(C)	C#	D	Eb	E	F#	G
Formula	1	2	#2(b3)	3	4	b5	5	6	b7

Shape 1:

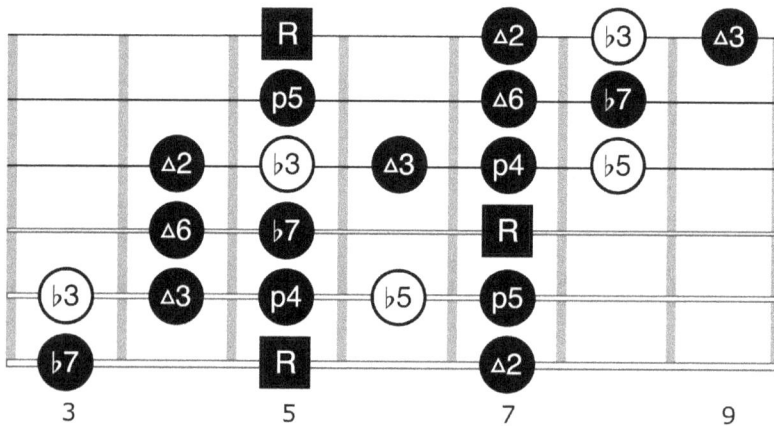

Shape 3:

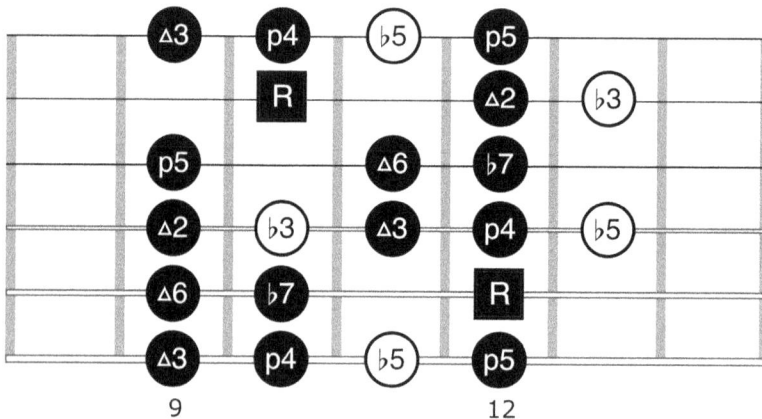

Shape 4:

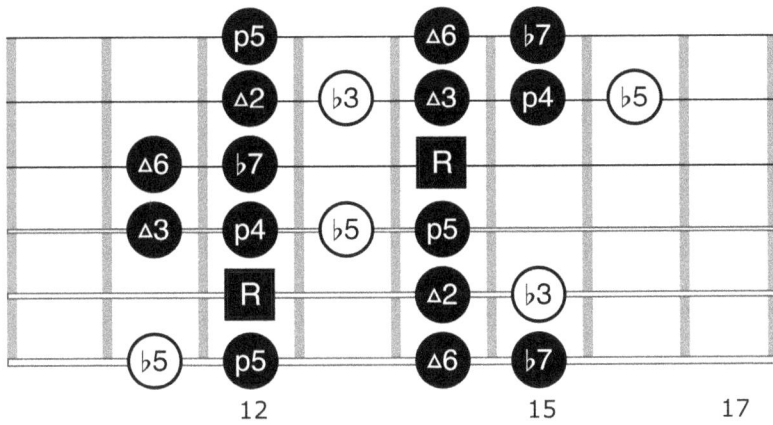

Although there are five different CAGED shapes, the three scale patterns shown above are enough to cover the entire neck for each dominant chord when transposed to the relevant root notes (A, D or E).

Extraction Process

Rather than fill this book with neck diagrams, it's better to get used to *extracting* different note combinations and flavours from the scale patterns you've already seen.

For example, if we extract the A Dominant Pentatonic scale (1, 2, 3, 5, b7) from within shape 4 of the A Mixolydian Blues Hybrid scale, it will look like this:

A Dominant Pentatonic Scale

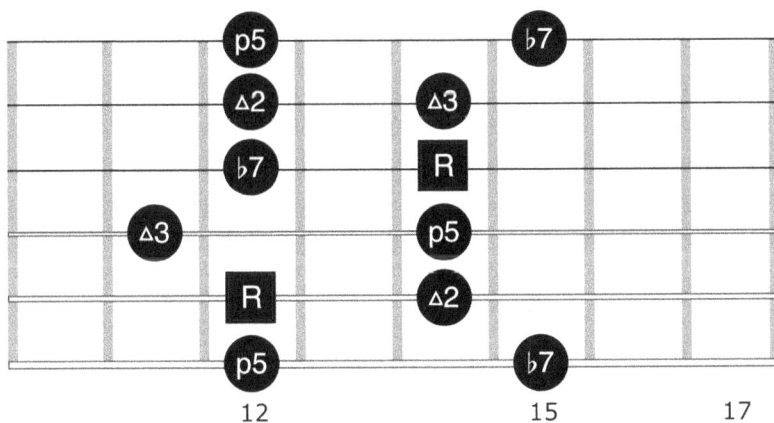

From this point forward, whenever a new scale is introduced, I will provide the interval formula. It's up to you to extract it from the Mixolydian Blues Hybrid scale. At first, you might find it useful to write out each new pattern as a visual reference.

Using the b3 Over Dominant Seventh Chords

Although technically incorrect, the minor third (b3) is often used to add a grittier quality over a dominant seventh chord, rather than the more conventional major third.

This note is commonly used in the following ways:

• With a 1/4-tone "curl" – a slight bend that stops somewhere between the minor and major third

• As a chromatic approach to the major third – bending or sliding into it from a semitone below

• As a bend from the 2nd note – used as a darker alternative to bending the 2nd up to the major third

Each approach adds a distinct blues flavour and will appear in various examples throughout the book.

Chromaticism

Chromatic notes (also known as non-scale tones) can be added in several useful ways. Here are three of the most important:

• Approach notes – typically a semitone below a scale note, often leading into a chord tone

• Bridging – inserting chromatic notes to connect one scale tone to another

• Enclosure – using at least one chromatic note to approach a target note from both above and below. A common example is approaching the major third of a dominant chord with a double chromatic movement: 4 to b3 to 3

In all transcriptions, chromatic notes are marked with an asterisk to make them easier to identify and study.

In general, I will label b3 and b5 as chromatic notes when played over a dominant seventh chord, unless they are part of a minor pentatonic or minor blues scale.

Musical Function

All of the implied progressions we will study follow certain musical principles. In short, they are valid substitutions that share the same function (or a close enough one) as the original chord. Because of this, it is not essential that every player on the bandstand approaches a section in exactly the same way. A keyboard player might outline one set of substitutions, while your lines are based on another. As long as both approaches relate logically to the original chord progression, they will work together musically.

Get the Audio

The audio files for this book are available to download for free from **www.fundamental-changes.com.** The link is in the top right-hand corner. Click on the "Guitar" link then simply select this book title from the drop-down menu and follow the instructions to get the audio.

We recommend that you download the files directly to your computer (not to your tablet or phone) and extract them there before adding them to your media library. If you encounter any difficulty, we provide technical support within 24 hours via the contact form.

For over 350 free guitar lessons with videos check out:

www.fundamental-changes.com

Join our free Facebook Community of Cool Musicians

www.facebook.com/groups/fundamentalguitar

Tag us for a share on Instagram: **FundamentalChanges**

Chapter One: Following the Basic Chords

The following four twelve-bar blues solos consolidate the three basic approaches outlined earlier, while also introducing more focused use of chord tones. These examples provide a solid foundation for developing a more advanced harmonic vocabulary.

The real test of your understanding is whether you can convey the sound of the chord progression when playing a solo – even without accompaniment. To do that, you need to learn how to target chord tones.

Each solo in this section places strong emphasis on outlining the notes of the underlying chords, while still maintaining enough stylistic character to sound like authentic blues. As you work through them, keep the following points in mind:

- *Thematic development* – look for variations on rhythms and melodic ideas to build musical cohesion

- *Space* – think about phrasing, not just continuous playing

- *Balance* – between different elements such as rhythmic variety, articulation, chord tone targeting, and the use of the minor blues scale

These concepts will appear throughout the book and are essential tools in developing a more expressive and harmonically rich blues soloing style.

Blues Solo #1

Bars Zero-Four

This solo begins with a strong sense of major tonality. The pick-up line moves from a grace note C to a C# (major 3rd of A7), before landing on the A root. From there, the next three bars are drawn from the A Minor Blues scale. Note how the C natural (minor 3rd) is often bent slightly upwards toward C#, hinting at the major 3rd without fully committing. This approach introduces tension while staying firmly within a blues context.

Bars Five-Six

Phrasing and thematic development are key here. The pick-up phrase from bar zero is echoed at the end of bar four, allowing the idea to continue just before the D7 arrives. The C# still works here because it is resolving back to a common tone: A, which is the root of A7 and the 5th of D7.

In bar six, the lick from bars 1–2 is revisited. Technically, the G natural doesn't fit neatly over the D7 chord (which contains an F#), but it still sounds convincing because the listener's ear is anchored to A as the tonal centre of the entire progression. Try replacing each G with F# to see how it feels. It may be more accurate harmonically, but does it still feel like the blues?

Bar Seven

This bar recalls the phrase from bar three, with a slight variation. It continues the theme and reinforces the call-and-response nature of the solo. The first four bars are now being developed and echoed through bars 5–8, creating a cohesive structure.

Bar Nine

Here, the line hovers between pure A Minor Blues and targeted chord tones. The D notes on beats 1, 2 and 3 outline the b7 of the E7 chord, but the C and Eb notes that surround them come straight from the A Minor Blues scale. They don't outline E7 specifically but serve the overall A blues tonality.

Bars Eleven-Twelve

This final section blends A7 arpeggio tones with elements of the A Minor Blues scale. The E7 is represented simply by a lone E note. In blues, the root note is often enough to imply the harmony, rather than spelling out more complex chord tones like the 3rd. Try finishing the solo on a G# instead (fret six on D string). It's theoretically correct, but does it feel right? These kinds of choices define your taste and help shape your personal voice on the instrument.

Blues Solo #1

Blues Solo #2

Bars One-Four

The first three bars are based on the A Major Blues scale (1, 2, b3, 3, 5, 6), which sits comfortably within the A Mixolydian Blues Hybrid scale introduced earlier in the book. In bar four, the solo shifts into A Minor Blues territory. Notice that the final few notes in bar four do not relate to A7. Instead, they anticipate the upcoming D7 chord in bars 5-6. This kind of early movement is a common device when soloing through changes. It avoids predictable phrasing and adds energy and forward motion to the line.

Bars Five-Six

These bars are built around the chord tones of D7 and use double-stops to emphasise harmony. Look at the first and fifth double-stops in bar five. The first features F# and D (the 3rd and root of D7), while the fifth features A and D (the 5th and root). These double-stops move chromatically between F# and A, while the D note acts as a pedal tone underneath, holding the harmony in place.

Bars Seven-Eight

Over the return to A7, we hear a repeated phrase in both bars which provides thematic development and a sense of cohesion. However, the phrase is rhythmically displaced in bar eight, giving it a different feel while still maintaining its identity.

Also notice the last note of bar eight – a G (the b7 of A7), which is bent up by a semitone to G# (the major 3rd of the following E7 chord). This kind of semitone movement into a key chord tone is a strong melodic choice. For example, when moving from A7 to D7, you might shift from G (b7 of A7) down to F# (3rd of D7). These small movements can make a big difference to how clearly the changes are outlined.

Bars Nine-Ten

This phrase over E7 is then moved down a whole tone and played again over D7, providing both rhythmic and melodic development. Look closely at how the notes target the chord tones of each respective chord.

Bars Eleven-Twelve

These final bars demonstrate that you don't need to outline every chord with its full arpeggio or scale. Over A7, the line combines A Mixolydian and A Minor Blues scale ideas. Over E7, a single E root note is enough to imply the change. This works because the E is also part of A7, but functions differently in the context of the E7 chord. The message here: clarity and economy can be just as effective as complexity.

Blues Solo #2

(Chromatic notes indicated by *)

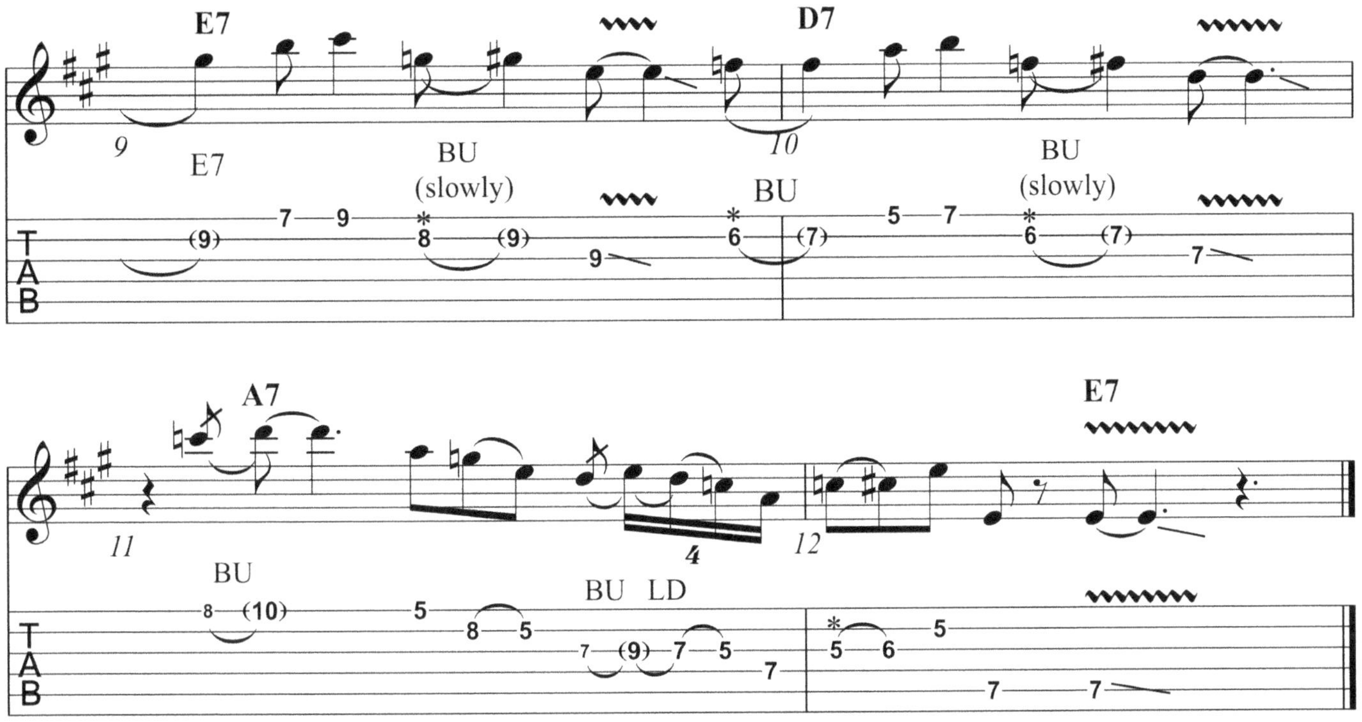
E7
D7
E7
BU
(slowly)
BU
BU
(slowly)
A7
E7
BU
BU LD

Blues Solo #3

Bars Zero-Two

Most of the notes in this opening section are drawn directly from an A7 arpeggio. The only exception is a C natural, which acts as a chromatic grace note into the C# (the 3rd of A7). This subtle detail adds a little grit to an otherwise harmonically clear outline.

Bar Three

Here, the line shifts into more traditional A Minor Pentatonic language, providing contrast with the arpeggio-based opening.

Bar Four

This bar features a variation on the original motif from bars 0-2. Instead of a C hammering on to C#, we hear a B hammering on to C, anticipating the D7 chord to come. C is the b7 of D7, so the phrase leads smoothly into the next section of the progression.

Bar Five-Seven

The modified version of the motif continues into the D7 chord. At the end of bar six, however, the phrase returns to its original form, anticipating the return to A7 in bar seven.

There's a clear structural repetition happening here: the ideas from bars 1-4 are echoed and reworked in bars 5–8. This use of motivic development brings unity and shape to the solo.

Bars Eight-Ten

The start of bar nine introduces a motif made entirely from E7 chord tones. It's preceded by a four-note run-up that anticipates the chord change, again showing how strong phrasing can outline harmony in advance. The same idea is repeated down a tone to reflect the D7 chord in the following bar.

Bars Ten-Eleven

Compositionally, these bars revisit the theme we first heard spanning bars 2-3 and 6–7, reinforcing the structural framework of the solo.

Bar Twelve

The final bar closes with an ascending chromatic figure leading to the E root. All of the notes in this line can be found within the A Minor Blues scale, giving the ending a satisfying and stylistically consistent resolution.

Blues Solo #3

(Chromatic notes indicated by *)

Blues Solo #4

This chorus takes inspiration from the blues tune *Hideaway* as played by Eric Clapton, but it's not meant to be an exact stylistic copy. It's more focused on the harmonic and melodic ideas involved, rather than tone, phrasing or vibrato.

Bars Zero-Eight

As with some of the earlier solos, these eight bars are divided into two parts: a four-bar idea repeated and modified to match the underlying chord changes.

Over A7, think of this section as being built from the A Major Blues scale with an added 4th (1, 2, b3, 3, 4, 5, 6). When the harmony shifts to D7, the major 3rd (C#) is dropped in favour of the minor 3rd (C). You could describe this as using D Mixolydian, but it's more helpful to hear it as a shift from a major to minor colour when viewed from the A tonal centre.

Bar Nine

This country-tinged line is drawn from E Mixolydian and most of the notes are strong chord tones from the E7 arpeggio.

Bar Twelve

The first seven notes spell out a D major triad, clearly outlining the underlying harmony. Even though the rest of the bar returns to an earlier motif, all but one of the notes are still part of D7, reinforcing the chord while maintaining musical continuity.

Bars Eleven-Twelve

These closing bars return to A7. Again, the focus is on strong chord tones, though the C natural (b3) appears more than once, subtly leaning back toward C# to create that classic blues tension.

As the solo wraps up, the only note used over E7 is the E root. It might seem sparse, but because E also appears in all the A-based scales used throughout the solo (Mixolydian, major blues, minor blues), it keeps things grounded and clear while still sounding authentic.

Blues Solo #4

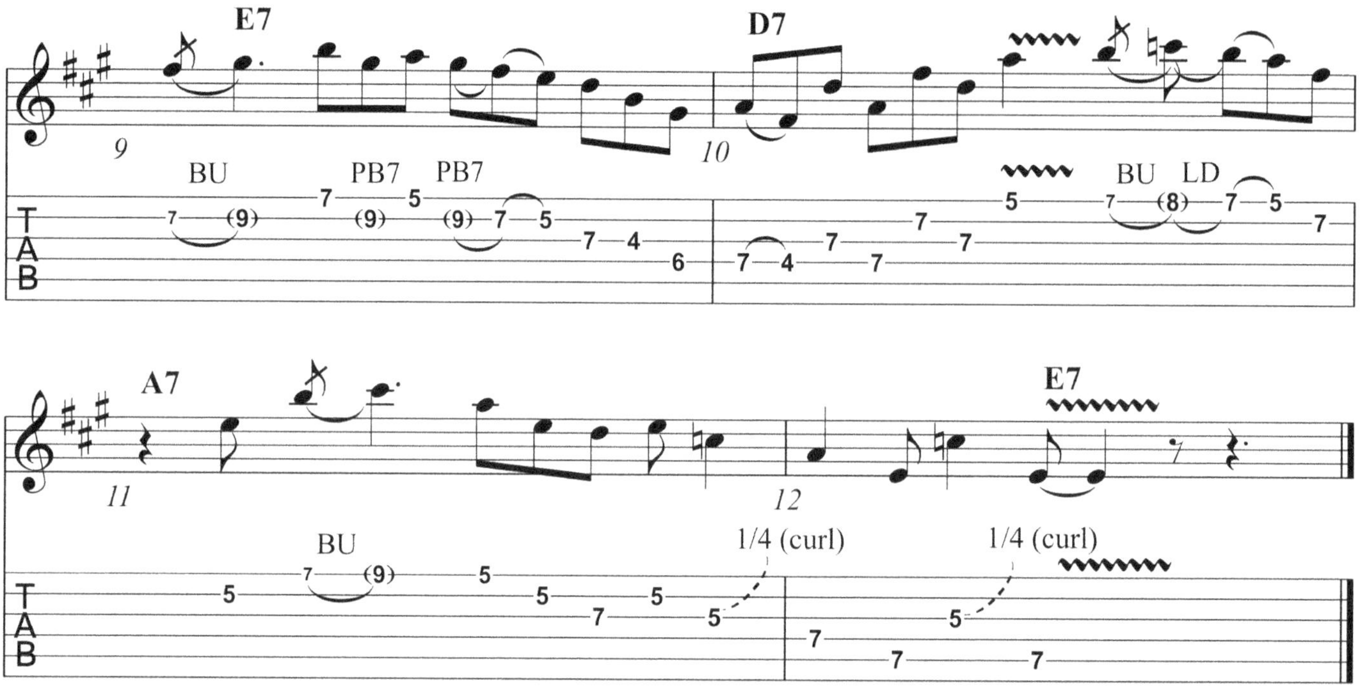
E7
D7
9
10
BU
PB7
PB7
BU
LD
A7
E7
11
12
BU
1/4 (curl)
1/4 (curl)
TAB

Chapter Two: Chord Substitutions

Perfect Cadence

Fundamentally, there are only a handful of chord types in Western music: major 7, dominant 7, minor 7, minor 7 flat 5, diminished 7, and altered dominant (7alt).

Of these six, two are dominant seventh chords but serve different functions.

Static vs Functional Dominant Sevenths

A dominant 7 chord is considered *static* when it doesn't push towards a resolution. For example, if you vamp on A7 for sixteen bars without it leading anywhere, the chord is acting in a static role. In this situation, A Mixolydian is the most consonant choice of scale. It includes all the chord tones (1, 3, 5, b7) and adds natural extensions (2, 4, and 6) without introducing any tension or instability.

1 (2) **3** (4) **5** (6) **b7**

Alternatively, a *functional* dominant 7 chord is one that forms part of a perfect cadence. This means it resolves to another chord a 4th higher (or a 5th lower). When this happens, the dominant 7 chord is referred to as a V7 chord because it sits on the fifth degree of the key and resolves to the tonic (I).

The V7 – I cadence is a cornerstone of Western harmony. It's the clearest musical expression of tension (V7) followed by release (I).

In the first four bars of a twelve-bar blues, the A7 chord could be viewed as *static* for the first three bars. In bar four, however, it begins to act *functionally* in that it leads up a 4th (or down a 5th) to a D chord in bar five.

This leads us to an important principle:

Any dominant seventh chord that resolves a 4th higher (or a 5th lower) can be altered, by adding b9, #9, b5 or #5 notes, to intensify the tension before resolving.

Note that when a b2 or #2 interval is added to a dominant seventh chord, those tones typically occur in the second octave and are therefore labelled b9 and #9 (e.g. A7b9, A7#9).

Our available chromatic tensions on a dominant seventh chord are limited to b2, #2, b5 and #5. These are the only gaps that exist within the Mixolydian scale. While there is also a gap between the b7 and the root, inserting a major 7th interval into that space would change the character of the chord from a dominant 7 to a major 7, which is a completely different sound.

1 (b2) **2** (#2) **3** **4** (b5) **5** (#5) **6** **b7**

This is essentially a kind of musical alchemy. If we are moving the listener from tension to resolution, we can heighten the tension on the V7 chord by altering it to 7#5, 7b5, 7b9, 7#9, 7#9#5 and so on, so that the eventual resolution to the settled-sounding I chord feels more satisfying.

This contrast creates a greater sense of drama and release. For this reason, the V7 chord often hosts some of the most colourful and expressive harmonic choices.

For example, if you know what an augmented triad is (1, 3, #5), but are unsure how to use it, now is the perfect opportunity. The augmented chord contains a major third and includes one of the available chromatic alterations (#5) that can be applied to a dominant chord to increase its tension.

I) A Augmented Triad (A+)

A Augmented Triad (A+)	A	C#	E#
Formula	1	3	#5

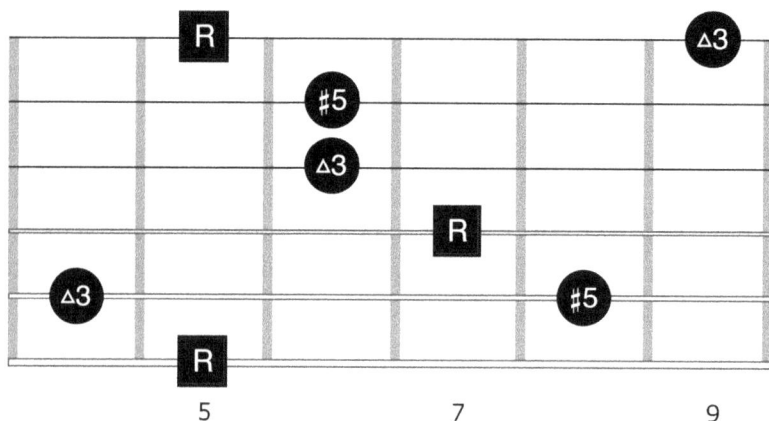

Example 2a demonstrates how the augmented triad shown in the previous diagram can be used to create tension in bar four. Notice how the tension built by the A+ arpeggio resolves into D Mixolydian over the D7 chord, landing primarily on chord tones that outline the new harmony.

D7	D	F#	A	C
Formula	1	3	5	b7

Example 2a

In the previous example, the A augmented triad filled the entire bar. However, especially at slower tempos, it's common to introduce the tension in just the second half of the bar to avoid it lingering for too long.

Example 2b uses A Minor Pentatonic in the first half of the bar, then moves to A+ in the second half. Notice how the transition between sounds is handled with a semitone shift, helping the line to flow smoothly and remain connected. This kind of voice leading helps to create a more natural musical narrative, rather than switching abruptly from one idea to another.

In all of the following examples, we'll begin with a familiar blues idea (using minor pentatonic, minor blues or Mixolydian) before introducing an altered dominant sound that resolves into chord tones of D7 (D, F#, A, C). Keep an eye on how those transitions are handled – they'll inform your own phrasing and help you to build stronger lines.

Example 2b

Here is another example using a different part of the same A+ triad shape.

Example 2c

In this next example, the F note on beat 4 of bar four is relocated from the 8th fret of the A string to the 3rd fret of the D string. This adjustment makes the line more comfortable to play without altering the note choice or phrasing.

Example 2d

Although we've just focused on one shape, you should also explore other positions and fingerings for the augmented triad. Bar four of Example 2e uses a series of major third intervals arranged higher up the neck, offering a fresh take on the same sound.

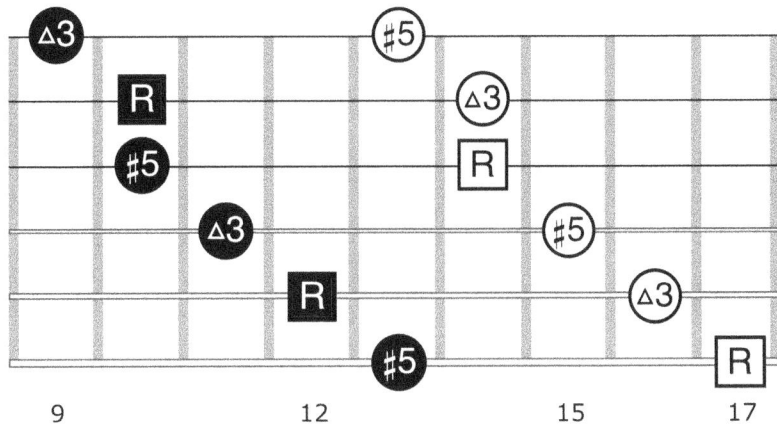

Example 2e

Again, note how the line resolves to chord tones of the D7 chord, in this case, F# and D, reinforcing the sound of the destination chord.

ii) The Augmented Scale

There are various scales from which an augmented triad can be built from its root. One of these is the Augmented scale.

A Augmented Scale	A	B#(C)	C#	E	E#(F)	G#
Formula	1	#2(b3)	3	5	#5(b6)	7

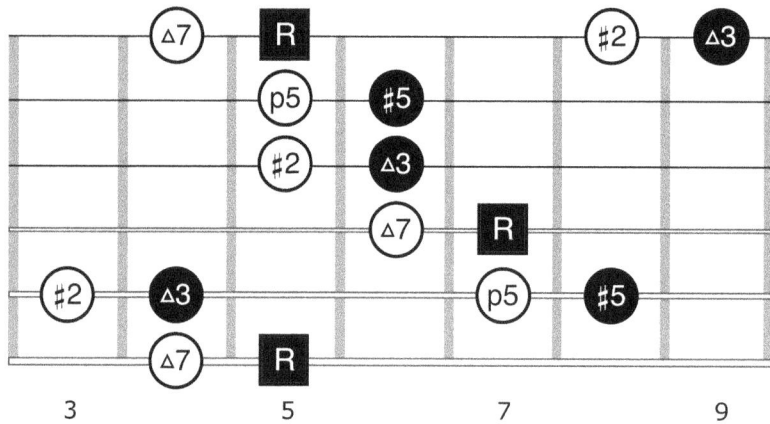

This six-note symmetrical scale can be viewed as two augmented triads a semitone apart. In this case, A augmented (A+, black notes in the diagram above) and G# augmented (G#+, white notes).

Although it doesn't contain a b7, the white notes can be used to pass chromatically into the black notes, which better suit the A7alt sound.

Our first example with this scale uses its symmetrical nature to create thematic and motivic development.

Example 2f

After the initial note in Example 2g, the phrase develops with a series of two-note figures that create a compelling "2 against 3" cross-rhythm when each pulse is divided into three notes.

Example 2g

A Augmented Scale

There's more symmetry on display in Example 2h, this time using double-stops to add a contrasting texture to the single-note lines used previously.

Example 2h

A Minor Pentatonic   A Aug. Scale

Example 2i features a greater variety of articulation, with less emphasis on symmetrical repetition.

Note that the line resolves to the D7 chord early, using a semitone bend to F# (the 3rd of D7) at the end of bar four. This note is tied over into bar five, where it is followed by an A (5th of D7).

Example 2i

So far, for ease of study, I've kept the examples in one area of the neck and used straight 1/8th notes. However, in this next one, a looser-sounding minor blues phrase is used in bar three to lead into the A Augmented scale idea in bar four.

Example 2j

iii) The Whole Tone Scale

Another six-note symmetrical scale that contains an augmented triad from its root is the whole tone scale.

A Wholetone Scale	A	B	C#	D#(Eb)	E#(F)	G
Formula	1	2	3	#4(b5)	#5(b6)	b7

This can be seen as being made up of two augmented triads a whole tone apart: A+ (black notes) and G+ (white notes). As with the previous scale, the black notes outline the triad that best matches the chord, while the white notes add contrast and tension.

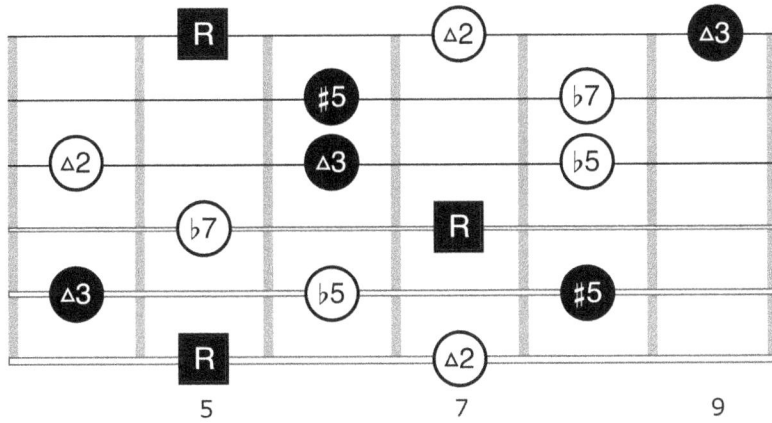

As a linear scale, the whole tone is made up entirely of consecutive tones (hence its name). It naturally lends itself to thematic development, as any whole tone idea can be moved up or down in whole steps without changing shape. Because of this, it features in many classic jazz patterns, but also turns up in well-known blues songs, such as the intro to *I Can Help* by Billy Swan.

Again, for ease of study, the following examples all use the same scale shape shown earlier, and each one sticks to a flow of consecutive 1/8th notes with no rests.

The first example features a straightforward ascent through the scale.

Example 2k

This idea moves third intervals through the scale, shifting them down in whole tones.

Example 2l

Next, we ascend an A+ triad and then descend a B+ triad. Again, note how this and the other examples feature a smooth transition from one scale to the next, often by just a semitone.

Example 2m

In this example, we have a mix of a three-note B+ triad followed by consecutive descending tones. Note how the phrase finishes by flowing into a higher position on the neck for the D7 resolution, allowing you to bend with the third finger on the 9th fret of the G string instead of using the first finger on the 5th fret of the B string.

Example 2n

A7 arpeggio

A Wholetone

Although we have confined our study to just one scale shape, you must explore other shapes and positions too. In this final whole tone example, we play a symmetrical series of augmented triads shifting down in tones on the neck.

Example 2o

D Minor Blues   D7

Iv) Superlocrian

When it comes to altered dominant scales, the daddy of them all is Superlocrian (also known as the Altered Scale). Apart from the root, major 3rd, and flat 7, it includes all four chromatic alterations: b2, # 2, b5, and #5.

A Superlocrian	A	Bb	(B#)C	(C#)Db	Eb	(E#)F	G
Formula	1	b2	(#2)b3	(3)b4	b5	(#5)b6	b7

It's the sort of scale that can seem impossible to use at first. This is because many self-taught guitarists grow up playing static sounds and haven't yet learned how to harness the power of a V7 chord. The opportunity to use this scale is specific and often very brief. Most players want to know what scale to use over an entire progression, but this particular sound is best applied in isolated moments.

As with the previous scales, the following examples are confined to one scale shape, use straight 1/8th notes, and are led into with a familiar blues phrase using minor pentatonic, minor blues or Mixolydian.

Once again, listen out for the semitone transitions that connect one scale to another.

Example 2p

Symmetrical relationships are always satisfying to spot, as they help us visualise the scale more clearly. In this case, we see a consecutive series of identical frets on each string at the end of bar four.

Example 2q

Although each scale is a potentially valuable source of ideas, it is important not to feel obligated to use every note. The following idea uses just four notes from A Superlocrian that could also be seen as being derived from A Whole Tone.

Example 2r

A7   D7

```
          5
T    5——8———————————5
A        7—(9)———8—7—5⁄6
B                          7
                    8——6⁄5—7⁄9
```
BU

        5   7
                                          7——9
                                    7——9

A Minor Blues Scale   A Superlocrian
                             or Wholetone

The previous examples started with A Minor Pentatonic. This one starts with A Mixolydian.

Example 2s

A7   D7

```
                              5——8⁄9—6
T              *——5—7——7              8——6—7——7    5—(8)—10
A          5—6                              8    7——7    7
B    5—7
```
BU

A Mixolydian   A Superlocrian

So far, the Superlocrian has been introduced in the second half of bar four, whereas in the following example, it is used throughout the entire bar to increase the tension.

The D Major Blues scale (1, 2, b3, 3, 5, 6) in bar five is just one of many different options that can be extracted from the D Mixolydian Blues Hybrid scale. A complete list of possibilities is provided in the conclusion of this book.

Example 2t

D Major Blues Scale

Finally, from a theoretical perspective, A Superlocrian is the seventh mode of the Bb Melodic Minor scale.

Bb Melodic Minor	Bb	C	Db	Eb	F	G	A
Formula	1	2	b3	4	5	6	7

I mention this because some players prefer to produce the sound of Superlocrian by playing Melodic Minor up a semitone from the root of an altered dominant chord. However, I do not recommend this dislocated way of thinking. Instead, I suggest learning to see the scale from the actual root note. This allows you to understand how each note functions in relation to the dominant seventh chord, and makes it easier to interchange with other altered dominant scales from the same root.

Half-Whole Scale

Not all altered dominant scales contain an augmented triad, however, and although it's not as flexible as Superlocrian, the Half-Whole scale is an eight-note symmetrical scale that deserves a mention. It is often used in **bar four** by blues players such as Robben Ford.

A Half-Whole Scale	A	Bb	B# (C)	C#	D# (Eb)	E	F#	G
Formula	1	b2	#2	3	#4/b5	5	6	b7

The scale is built from alternating semitones and whole tones (hence its name), and like the Whole Tone scale, its symmetry lends itself well to thematic development. As such, it is a common source of material for many classic jazz phrases.

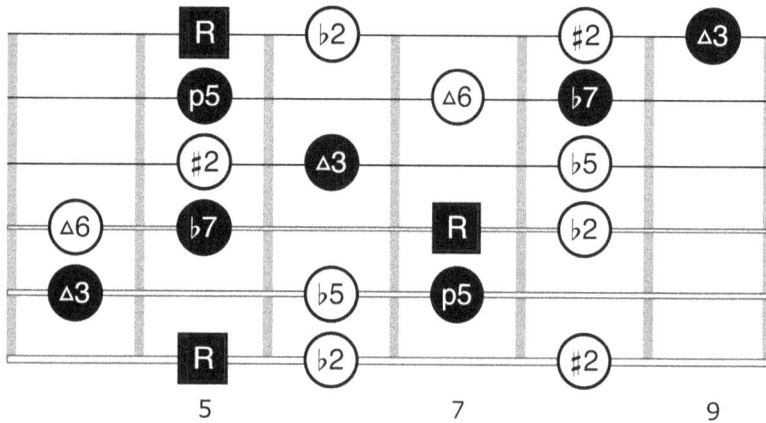

Just look at all the different triads and arpeggios that can be played from an A root (A, Am, A°, A7, A7b5, A6 etc)! Because this symmetrical scale repeats every four frets, any of these shapes can also be played from C, Eb, and F#.

One of the most useful triads is the major one built from the sixth note of the scale (F#). Although it's just a simple F# major triad (1, 3, 5 from F#), when viewed from A, the notes become 3, 6 (13), and b2 (b9). This creates a strong A13b9 sound when played against an A7 chord.

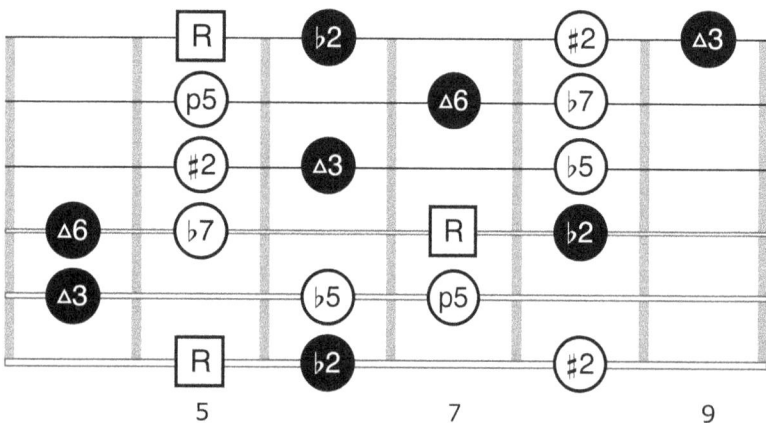

The following two-line examples show this triad being used in the second half of bar four. In the first one, the F# triad takes up the last two beats of the bar.

Example 2u

A Minor Blues scale   F#

Whereas, in Example 2v, we use only three notes from the F# triad at the very end (last beat) – just enough to state the full triad.

Example 2v

A Mixolydian   F#

Within the original Half-Whole scale shape (above), you can see the notes of a dominant 7 arpeggio (1, 3, 5, b7) shown in black.

By replacing each root note with a b2 (b9), you create an important arpeggio sound that we'll explore in more detail in the next chapter. For now, simply think of it as an A7b9 arpeggio without the root.

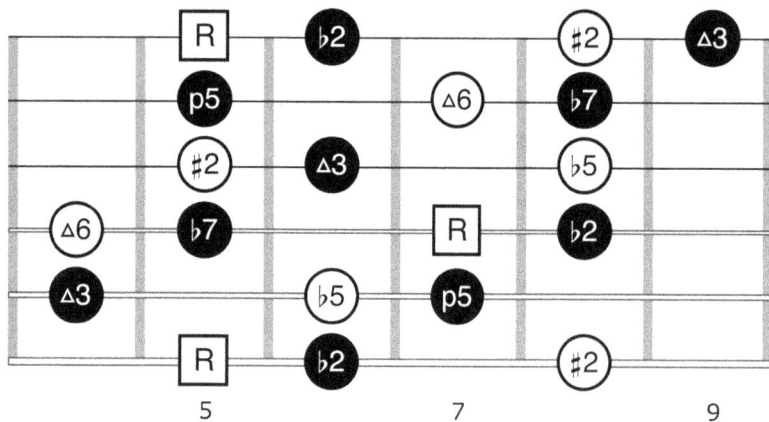

Example 2w

A Minor Pentatonic   A7b9 (no root)   D Maj. Pent.

Example 2x draws upon the symmetrical properties of the Half-Whole scale. Bar four begins with a four-note motif (A7b5), which is then moved down in minor 3rd intervals, giving us F#7b5 and Eb7b5 respectively.

This wholesale movement would be more obvious if we simply shifted the first four notes down four frets each time, but in this example the motif is adapted to stay within a single vertical shape, allowing us to remain in the same position on the neck.

Finally, playing groups of four notes against a triplet count creates an interesting "3 against 4" rhythmic feel.

Example 2x

A Half-Whole

As before, although we have focused on just one scale pattern, it's important that you explore other patterns in different areas of the neck.

The following example descends laterally and features a high level of contrast by using two triads from within the scale that share no common tones – a concept known as a triad pair. Here, we alternate between A and Eb, although another useful triad pair found within A Half-Whole is F# and C.

Example 2y

Even though some altered dominant scales do not contain all the possible chromatic alterations (for example, the Whole Tone has no b2 or #2, and Half-Whole has no #5), it is still worth exploring each type, as they each offer a unique symmetry and flavour.

The Phrygian Dominant scale (1, b2, 3, 4, 5, b6, b7 – the fifth mode of Harmonic Minor), for instance, can create a more ethnic sound, adding a Gypsy or Latin-tinged character to your lines.

Finally, remember that all the principles covered in this chapter can also be applied to the E7 chord in bar twelve. Since it functions as a V7 leading back to A7 (the first bar of the next chorus), any altered dominant ideas you've developed for bar four can be transposed to this spot as well.

Tritone Substitution (Side-Slipping)

If you've listened to much blues, you may have noticed how accompanists will often introduce a chord by briefly playing the same chord a semitone higher. This technique (also used in funk and jazz) is known as side-slipping and it can also be applied to lines.

The reason it works is because the side-slip chord functions like a highly altered V7 chord.

For example, if we play an Eb7 or Eb9 at the end of bar four to introduce the D7 or D9 in bar five, that Eb chord can be viewed not just as a chord from Eb, but as a tension-filled sound that resolves nicely to D, and which therefore also relates to A.

Eb9 Seen From An A Root Note

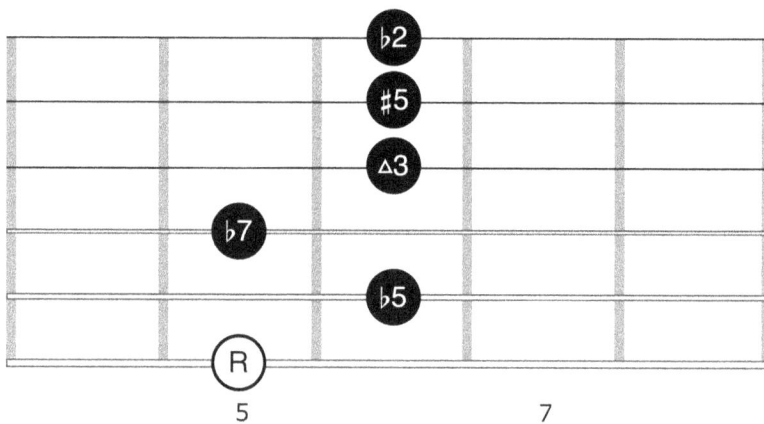

Rule: A dominant chord followed by another a 4th higher (or 5th lower) can be substituted by a dominant chord whose root is a b5 away.

This is known as a Tritone Substitution or b5 Substitution.

As with the previous altered dominant scale examples, a tritone substitution featuring Eb7 is used in the second half of bar four in the following example.

Example 2z

Note how, in both the previous and following line, the tension resolves early to the D7 chord.

Example 2z1

Tritone substitution principles allow us to precede the chord at the start of each bar with a dominant 7 chord a semitone above.

Technically, it is possible to fill an entire twelve-bar blues sequence with tritone substitution (side-slipping) moves:

(A7)	(Bb7)	(A7)	(Bb7)	(A7)	(Bb7)	(A7)	(Eb7)
A7							

(D7)	(Eb7)	(D7)	(Bb7)	(A7)	(Bb7)	(A7)	(F7)
D7				**A7**			

(E7)	(Eb7)	(D7)	(Bb7)	(A7)	(F7)	(E7)	(Bb7)
E7		**D7**		**A7**		**E7**	

The scheme above shows chords changing every two beats. While this is an interesting way to practice (and commonly used in jazz), we won't be looking at examples of it here, as it tends to sound over-written and very unlike the blues.

Instead, think of it as an effect to draw on occasionally. Use it sparingly and with plenty of vocal-style articulation to help it sound more earthy and natural.

Major ii – V – Is

One common development of the perfect cadence (V7 to I) is to expand it into a ii – V – I.

This progression works well because the ii chord (usually a minor 7) functions as a suspended version of the V7 chord:

iim7 – V7 – I = V7sus4 – V7 – I

Earlier, we discussed how many musicians like to introduce tension in the second half of a bar, especially at slower tempos. This is where a ii – V – I becomes particularly useful.

Playing Em7 to A7alt in bar four, rather than holding A7alt for the entire bar, allows the tension to unfold more naturally rather than dragging it out too long.

In this case, Em7 is functionally equivalent to the upper four notes of A9sus4.

Em7	E	G	B	D	
Formula	1	b3	5	b7	

A9sus4	A	D	E	G	B
Formula	1	4	5	b7	9

In bar four of the following examples, the Em9 arpeggio shape shown below is used over the Em7 in each implied major ii – V – I line.

Em9 Arpeggio

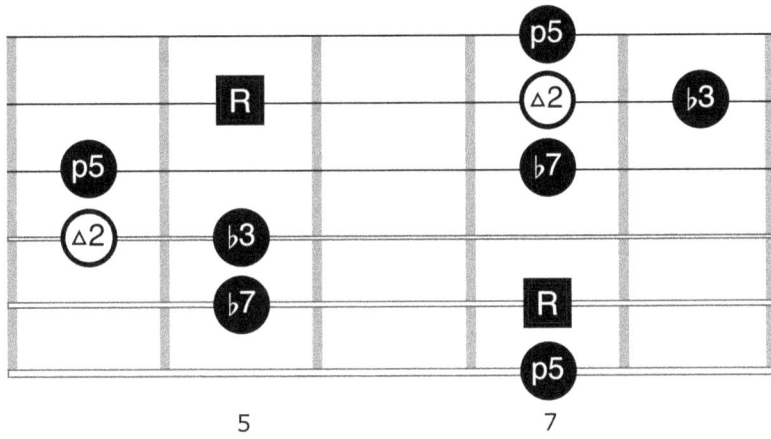

The first two lines use a familiar A Minor Pentatonic phrase to set things up from bar three. Each Em9 idea in the first half of bar four is followed by an A Superlocrian line using Shape 1 over the implied A7alt (V7), which then leads to and resolves on D7 in bar five.

Example 2z2

Example 2z3

The next two examples use the A Half-Whole scale over the implied A7alt (V7).

In one of them, you'll see a two-octave F# major triad which, as mentioned earlier, outlines an A13b9 sound when played against the A7 chord.

Example 2z4

The following example uses the A7b9 rootless arpeggio demonstrated earlier. Note how it resolves early to D7 using a chord tone (A), which is shared by both A7 and D7.

Example 2z5

Em9 arpeggio

A7b9 no root

All the previous examples stuck closely to the same scale shapes, but you should also explore the fingering possibilities offered by playing the same arpeggios and their associated scales in other areas of the neck.

In this next example, we begin in CAGED Shape 4 of E Dorian (over the implied Em7), before using a small fragment of an F# triad (from A Half-Whole) over the implied A7alt chord.

Example 2z6

Finally, make sure to transpose all ideas from Em7, A7, D7 in bars 4-5 up seven frets (or down five frets if more practical) to Bm7, E7, A7 for the transition from bar twelve into bar one.

Chapter Three: Diminished Seventh Substitution

In bar six of a 12-bar blues in A, it's common to play a D# diminished seventh chord. This creates a smooth chromatic bass movement from D to D# to E, with E acting as the fifth of the A7 chord that follows.

D7   D#o7   A7 (2nd inv.)

A diminished 7 chord (1, b3, b5, bb7) is perfectly symmetrical and repeats in minor 3rd intervals (four frets). The four chords below all contain the same notes, just in a different order:

D#°7 = F#°7 = A°7 = C°7

You'll notice that D#°7 can be interpreted as a D7 chord with a b2 (b9) in the bass instead of the root. In other words, it's an inversion of a D7b9 chord.

D#°7 = F#°7 = A°7 = C°7

can also be viewed as:

D7b9 = F7b9 = G#7b9 = B7b9

Personally, I find it more helpful to reinterpret diminished 7 chords as 7b9 chords. By treating D#°7 as D7b9, we can continue to think of things from a D root note over the D7 chord. This offers a more intuitive and musically relevant approach for bar six of our twelve-bar progression.

Example 3a uses the following scale and arpeggio shapes for bars 5-6.

D Mixolydian / D Lydian b7 / D7b9

Note that we don't need to imply the D#°7 right from the start of bar six. Here, it's introduced in the second half of the bar to keep the tension brief and more effective.

Example 3a

The scale normally associated with a diminished 7 chord is the Diminished scale – an eight-note symmetrical pattern made up of alternating whole steps and half steps (also called the Whole-Half scale).

In fact, the D# Whole-Half scale contains exactly the same notes as the D Half-Whole scale – they're just modes of one another – which means we can use the same useful shortcut as before and think in terms of D7b9 (D Half-Whole) rather than D#°7 (D# Half-Whole).

This next line uses a D Half-Whole scale shape in bar six before resolving to chord tones of A7 in bar seven.

D Half-Whole Scale

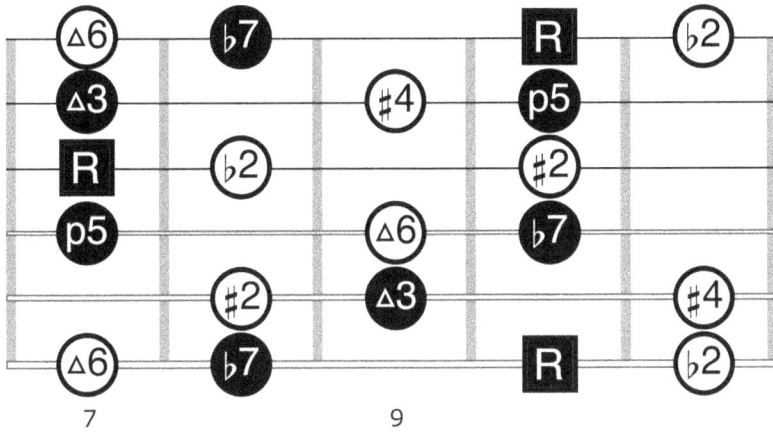

Example 3b

This chapter has demonstrated an important substitution concept that will be used extensively in later examples and solos. In the next chapter we'll look at the blues turnaround.

Chapter Four: The Blues Turnaround

A turnaround is the name given to the final two bars of the 12-bar blues form. It's the part of the sequence that naturally leads the listener back to the start.

Using Common Scales From A

There are many ways to approach this section, and we'll begin with some ideas based on different A-rooted scales. In each case, the line resolves to an E note in bar twelve to reflect the underlying E7 chord. This mirrors the kind of resolution we've already seen in the earlier solo studies.

The first two lines use five-note scales.

This one uses the Am6 Pentatonic scale (1, b3, 4, 5, 6), which is another sound found within the A Mixolydian Blues Hybrid scale.

Am6 Pentatonic Scale	A	C	D	E	F#
Formula	1	b3	4	5	6

Example 4a

(Am6 Pentatonic)

The A Major Pentatonic scale (1, 2, 3, 5, 6) is another option.

A Major Pentatonic Scale	A	B	C#	E	F#
Formula	1	2	3	5	6

Example 4b

(A Major Pentatonic scale)

This next example uses the six-note A Minor Blues scale (1, b3, 4, b5, 5, b7) and is reminiscent of players like Gary Moore.

Example 4c

(Gary Moore Minor Blues scale)

The following four examples all use a mixture of scales extracted from the nine-note A Mixolydian Blues Hybrid parent scale. Again, for a full reference of these scales, see the table at the end of the book.

Example 4d

If we play A Mixolydian with a minor 3rd instead of a major 3rd (C instead of a C#) we get A Dorian.

Example 4e

A Dorian

A Major Triad
(A Major Pentatonic or A Mixolydian)

Although shown as three separate scales, every note of the following example can be found within the A Mixolydian Blues Hybrid scale.

Example 4f

A Mixolydian

A Minor Blues

A Major triad

Although the C note below is marked with an asterisk to indicate a chromatic note, the last six notes in bar eleven could all be interpreted as part of the A Major Blues scale (1, 2, b3, 3, 5, 6).

Example 4g

A Mixolydian

A Major Pentatonic

Next, we're going to look at implying various cadences (chord progressions) in bar eleven to add interest and harmonic direction to our lines.

Turnaround Cadences (Chord Motion)

Harmonically, the last two bars of the blues can be expanded from this:

A7	E7
11	12

To this:

A (A7) (D) (D#o7)	A (F 7) E7
11	12

The first five chords represent a compressed version of the changes commonly played or implied in bars 3-7, tied together by a chromatically ascending bass motion. This type of movement forms the basis of many classic blues turnaround lines.

We'll now look at line examples that stem from this implied sequence and explore some variations on it. As you work through each one, analyse how the notes relate to the implied chords shown in brackets. After that, try writing your own lines using the same principles.

A, A7, D7, D#°7

At first glance, bar eleven of the next example could seem like standard A7 blues playing, but every note in the line outlines the underlying chords.

Example 4h

This next idea shows just one of the many other ways to outline the same chords. Note the use of hammer-ons, slides, curls, pull-offs and vibrato in a short phrase to add expression and keep the listener's ear engaged.

Example 4i

A, A7, D, Dm

In this first variation, Dm (D, F, A) acts like the 4, b7 and b9 of an E7b9sus, creating a strong pull toward the A7 through a classic V – I resolution.

E7b9sus4	E	A	B	D	F
Formula	1	4	5	b7	b9

Again, analyse the notes of each of the following lines against the series of implied chords shown in brackets. From the second beat of the following two ideas, there is chromatic descending motion on the lower string.

Example 4j

```
A7                                                    E7 wwww
    11
   (A)      (A7)      (D)      (Dm)     (A7)       (E7)
                               Hold----------------|

T---------------5-------3-------3------2---------------------
A-------6-------------------------------2----------------7---
B---7-------7\5---5\4------4\3-----3------3----5---6*--6--7---
                                                  5   6  7
```

In this one, there is a high A pedal on the B string throughout bar eleven.

Example 4k

```
A7                                                   E7 wwww
    11                                    12
   (A)     (A7)      (D)     (Dm)        (A7)      (E7)
Ring-----------------------------------------------------------------|

T------------10--------10-------10---------------------------
A------------------------------------------------------7-----
B---12--12--10----10--9-----9--8------8\7----5--6*--6--7-----
                                                  5   6  7
   П    П   П  m  П  П  m  П   П  m  П
```

Passing notes to E,
or A Minor Blues scale

In this example, note how predictability is avoided by leaving a rest at the start and then pushing early at the end of bar eleven into the A7 of the following bar. Try to look for the same approach in the next few examples as well.

Example 4l

Here's a variation on the same scheme used in the previous line.

Example 4m

Like many of the previous examples, this next one has enough blues-style articulation to stop it sounding too academic or sterile. Again, notice how we push into the E note that relates to A7 at the end of bar eleven to avoid things sounding too square.

Example 4n

A, A7, D7, F7

Here's another variation on the basic sequence, shown here using chord symbols.

And here's a different version of it that is often visualised when playing single-note lines.

This variation is derived from A, A7, D7, D#°7, and can be reinterpreted using diminished theory i.e., F7b9 functions as a substitute for D#°7.

B7b9 = D7b9 = F7b9 = Ab7 is equivalent to D#°7 = F#°7 = A°7 = C°7

This kind of cadence allows for contrary motion, where chord tones or lines move in opposite directions to create strong harmonic interest.

And it's this same contrary motion that forms the basis of the following example, which also features a pedal on the root note (A at the 10th fret of the B string).

Example 4o

A, A7, Ab7, G7

This is the last of our commonly implied turnaround cadences. It has a distinctive chromatic character and a strong sense of movement.

A7 ... E7

(A)   (A7)   (Ab7)   (G7)   (A7)   (E7)

```
    5     5     4     3     3
T   5     5     4     3     2           5
A   6     6     5     4     2           7
B   7     5     4     3     0           6
    7     7     6     5                 7
    5     5     4     3
```

And here's the same sequence, this time using inversions that lend themselves well to single-note line construction. These voicings offer smoother movement across the fretboard and can help you to build more fluid, connected phrases.

A7 ... E7

(A)   (A7)   (Ab7)   (G7)   (A7)   (E7)

```
    5     9     8     7     5
T   5     8     7     6     5           5
A   6     9     8     7     6           7
    7     7     6     5     5           6
                                        7
```

This turnaround variation is based on the progression A, A7, D7, Dm and works because:

Ab7 functions as a tritone substitution for D7.

G7 can be understood as an inversion of Dm   specifically as Dm6/11.

Together, they create a classic descending chromatic line that's both symmetrical and instantly recognisable in countless blues and jazz settings.

Example 4p

Note how variety is introduced in this next example by starting on beat 2 instead of right at the beginning of the bar. This slight rhythmic shift helps keep things fresh and avoids predictability. Look at the similarity between this line and Example 4j. Both feed off the underlying chords, but this one is more symmetrical and chromatic.

Example 4q

This final example features chromatically descending double-stops with a repeating A pedal on the top E string.

Example 4r

Here are some other possible turnaround cadences for you to imply and explore:

A, C7, B7, Bb7

A, Eb7, D7, C#7

By applying diminished theory, the second variation above has moved the last three chords of the previous variation up a minor third. All these variations are built from the same underlying progression and serve as valid substitutions, sharing the same harmonic function.

At the core of every example lies a perfect cadence. Each cadence in this chapter relates in some way to the Cycle of 5ths, where V7 chords are linked together in sequence.

For instance, if we take the earlier example of A, C7, B7, Bb7 and apply tritone substitutions to the second and fourth chords, we get F#7 and E7 respectively. The resulting sequence is a staple of jazz blues:

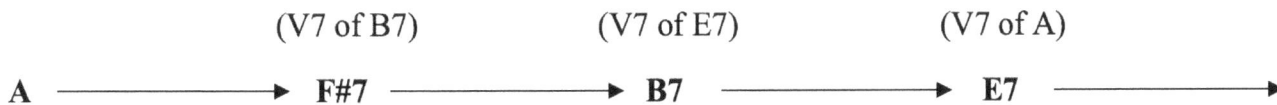

Remember that, because each cadence variation functions in a similar way, the members of a band do not all need to play the same changes.

The following two 12-bar solos demonstrate how some of the chord-tone-based turnaround cadences we've just explored can be implied in a soloing context.

Blues Solo #5

Tonally, the bulk of this solo hovers between A dominant for the A7 and A minor for the other chords. However, the chord tones of the underlying changes are consistently targeted.

There are a few notable details. First, the pick-up line at the end of bar six is played in anticipation of the A7 chord. Technically, the C# clashes with the D7 underneath, but because the following chord is so clearly implied (and because the note is part of the main musical motif), it still works. Try substituting that C# with a D (the root of D7) and decide for yourself which version feels more musical. Is it more important to outline the chord you're on, or to express the broader tonal centre of the progression?

Bars Eleven-Twelve

Bar eleven features a descending line of chromatic sixth intervals, outlining the familiar A, A7, Ab7, G blues-style turnaround.

In bar twelve, the line resolves to A7 before ascending chromatically to finish on a clean E7 chord.

Blues Solo #5

E7   D7

A7   E7

Blues Solo #6

First Four Bars

This section features classic A7-based vocabulary, built around chord tones with a touch of the usual C/C# tension. The end of bar four anticipates bar five and targets D7 instead of A7. This works because the harmonic tension at the end of bar four is resolved by the arrival of the D7 chord in bar five.

Bars Five-Six

These bars continue the theme of targeting chord tones, this time relating to D7. As before, the end of bar six leads us smoothly into bar seven, anticipating the return to A7.

Bar Nine

Here we get into a matter of taste. The held double-stop is drawn from the A Minor Blues scale and contains an E note (5th of A7, root of E7) and a G note (b7 of A7, but a b3 interval over E7). You could swap the G for a G# to make it more "correct" but listen carefully and decide whether that version sounds too polished. A little grit can go a long way.

Bars Eleven-Twelve

We hear a chromatic climb on the G string against an A pedal on the top E string. These notes follow the familiar A, A7, D, D#°7 turnaround and resolve neatly to the fifth of A7 (E) in bar twelve.

To finish, there's a side-slip from F7 to E7. Thanks to tritone substitution, F7 acts like an altered B7, which is the V7 of E. This movement creates strong tension and release at the end of the solo.

Blues Solo #6

Using Altered Dominant Scales

Common A-root Scales in Bar Eleven and an E Altered Dominant Scale in Bar Twelve

The following examples show how to anticipate the arrival of the E7 chord by introducing E altered dominant sounds from the start of bar twelve, rather than waiting until the second half.

This early move into altered territory helps to create forward momentum, urgency, and a stronger pull towards the resolution. As always, the effectiveness of this technique will depend on the tempo and intensity of the musical setting.

This first example uses a straight ascending E+ triad.

E Augmented Triad (E+)	E	G#	B#(C)
Formula	1	3	#5

Example 4s

A Minor Blues

E+

Example 4t uses the following shape for the E Augmented scale in bar twelve.

E Augmented Scale	E	F##(G)	G#	B	B#(C)	D#
Formula	1	#2(b3)	3	5	#5(b6)	7

E Augmented Scale CAGED Shape 5

Example 4t

A Major Pentatonic

E Augmented scale

The following example uses the E Whole Tone scale in bar twelve, built from consecutive whole steps. This symmetry gives it a smooth, floating quality and makes it easy to shift ideas up or down by a tone without changing fingering.

E Whole Tone Scale	E	F#	G#	A#(Bb)	B#(C)	D
Formula	1	2	3	#4(b5)	#5(b6)	b7

Example 4u

A Major Pentatonic

E Whole-Tone scale

A

Try experimenting with ideas using other altered dominant scales in bar twelve, such as E Superlocrian and E Half-Whole. Each offers its own flavour of tension, so explore how they sound and resolve differently into A7.

This final example presents a well-balanced blend of approaches. We begin by outlining the chord tones of an implied turnaround cadence in bar eleven, then shift between A7 and an E altered dominant flavours using the Whole Tone scale. It offers a melodic contrast to simply running through the A Minor Blues scale alone – not that there's anything wrong with that, of course!

Example 4v

Some modern, blues-influenced fusion and jazz players, such as John Scofield, like to use A or E altered dominant scales throughout bars eleven and twelve. This can work well, especially at faster tempos, where any tension created is short-lived and quickly resolved.

Finally, you might already play some classic blues turnaround lines without fully understanding the harmonic thinking behind them. Hopefully, with the concepts and cadences we've explored in this chapter, you'll now be able to unpack those lines and connect them to the underlying harmonic ideas they imply.

Chapter Five: Other Advanced Concepts

Implying Minor ii – V – Is

A Minor ii – V – I progression typically starts with a minor 7b5 chord and resolves to a minor i chord.

Interestingly, the chords of the sequence D7 – D#°7 – A7 in bars 5-7 can be viewed as inversions of a minor ii – V – I progression – in this case: F#m7b5 – B7b9 – Em6.

ii (F#m7b5)	V (B7b9)	I (Em6)	
D7	(D#o7)	A7	
5	6	7	8

F#m7b5 functions like a first inversion D9 (with the 3rd in the bass).

D#°7 can be interpreted as D7 with a b9 in the bass (D7b9 = F7b9 = Ab7b9 = B7b9).

Em6 works like a second inversion A9 (with the 5th in the bass).

Understanding these equivalences gives you more creative freedom when constructing lines, and highlights how closely the major and minor cadences can be intertwined in a blues context.

This fresh perspective will cause you to play different ideas than just thinking D7, D#°7, A7.

The following line is based around these arpeggio shapes.

F#m7b5, B7(b9), Em6

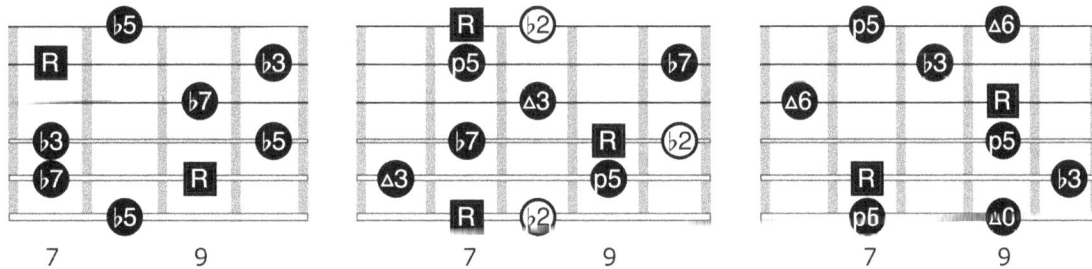

Note that we are not including the b9 over the implied B7b9 chord here. Instead, we are outlining a plain B7 sound to keep things simpler and more grounded.

Example 5a

Short Minor ii – V – I (F#m7b5, B7b9, Em7) in Bars 6-7

Because the D#°7 in bar six is implied rather than stated, we can choose to extend the D7 through that bar if we wish. This allows us to compress the implied minor ii – V – I progression into bar six instead of stretching it across bars 5-6.

The following line uses the same arpeggio shapes as the previous example but fits them into a shorter space to reflect this compressed version.

Example 5b

A7

(Em6)

The following two examples use a different fingering of the same arpeggios, now played in and around the 5th to 7th, rather than the 7th to 9th fret area.

F#m7b5, B7(b9), Em6

Example 5c

D7

(D#o7)

(F#m7b5)

(B7b9)

D Mixolydian

A7

(Em6)

A Mixolydian

In the following example, note the double chromaticism leading into the F# (5th of the implied B7b9) in bar six.

Example 5d

D7

(D#o7)

5

BU   BU

(F#m7b5)   (B7b9)

D Mixolydian

A7

7   *8*

(Em6)

A Minor Pentatonic

Improvising over a minor ii – V – I is not limited to simply outlining each arpeggio. By visualising F#m7b5, B7b9 and Em6 instead of D7, D#o7 and A7, we gain access to a broader palette of tonal colours, including various altered dominant scales over the implied B7b9.

The following example adopts a more scalic approach over each chord, while still placing strong emphasis on chord tones (shown in black).

F#m7b5 (F# Locrian), B7#5 (B Superlocrian), Em6 (E Dorian)

Example 5e

D Mixolydian

A Major Blues Scale

E Dorian contains the same notes as A Mixolydian but presents a different tonal focus. In this example, the ideas from the second half of bar seven signal a return to A7, expressed through the A Major Blues scale (1, 2, b3, 3, 5, 6).

Short Minor ii – V – I (C#m7b5, F#7b9, Bm7) in Bars 4-5

Just as every major chord has a relative minor four frets lower (e.g., C and Am), every major ii – V – I has a corresponding minor ii – V – I the same interval below.

For instance, the major ii – V – I progression Em7 – A7b9 – D, which is implied in bars 4-5 (see the end of Chapter Two) has a relative minor ii – V – i of C#m7b5 – F#7b9 – Bm7.

These substitutions work because of the significant note overlap between the chords:

• Em7 (when viewed as a slash chord, C#m7b5 = Em/C#)

• A7b9 (via diminished theory, F#7b9 = A7b9 = C7b9 = D#7b9)

• D (when expressed as a slash chord, Bm7 = D/B)

In the following example, the F#m7b5, B7b9, Em6 idea from bars 6-7 of the earlier phrase has been transposed up seven frets to imply a C#m7b5, F#7b9, Bm7 progression in bars 4-5, with a modified ending.

Example 5f

Again, although it shares many of the same notes as its relative major ii – V – I, thinking in terms of the related minor ii – V – I offers a different visual perspective on the fretboard and will naturally lead you towards different musical ideas.

"Quick Change" In Bar Two

Many blues tunes briefly shift to the IV chord (D7) in bar two. This is known as a "quick change".

This is something that can be implied whether the rest of the band play it or not, as it falls in a weak (even-numbered) bar, and any tension created can be resolved naturally back to A7 in bar three.

With the implied D7, bars 2-3 become a miniature version of bars 5-8, allowing us to play a compressed version of the D7, D#°7, A7 sequence we often outline in that section.

(A7)   (D7)   (D#o7)   (A7)

A7			
1	2	3	4

Example 5g

Hold---| (D7)   (D#o7)   (A7)   Hold---|

A Mixolydian   A Mixolydian

This change can be compressed even further so that it appears in the second half of that bar.

(A) (A7) (D7) (D#o7) (A7)

A7			
1	2	3	4

The eagle-eyed among you will have noticed that this combination of chords is the same as one of the turnaround cadence options we've explored for bar eleven. Try playing any bar eleven ideas from Chapter Four over bar two using the backing track.

Bar two of the following example is the same as bar eleven from Example 4h and is followed in bar three by a modified version of what happened in bar twelve of the original.

The critical difference between bar two and bar eleven is that we are now leading into this implied turnaround cadence with notes that relate to A7 (bar one), not D7 (bar ten).

Example 5h

A Dorian

A Minor Pentatonic

Unlike bar twelve, bar three doesn't need to target an E7 chord, although you could imply one if you resolve it to the I chord (A7) in bar four. Bar two of the next example is the same as bar eleven from Example 4i.

Example 5i

A Mixolydian

What's more, because they share the same harmonic principles, you can also apply any of those bar eleven turnaround cadences in bar three. For example:

	(A) (A7) (D7) (Dm)	(A7)	
A7			
1	2	3	4

Here, bar two contains the same A, A7, D, Dm-based line used in bar eleven of Example 4j.

Example 5j

Bar two of the next example contains the same line used in bar eleven of Example 4l. Again, bar three contains a modified version of bar twelve of the original. Here it resolves to A7 instead of E7.

Example 5k

A Minor 6 Pentatonic

A Dorian

Also, earlier in this chapter, we saw that the cadence implied in bars 5-7 (D7, D#°7, A7) can be viewed as an inversion of a minor ii – V – I (F#m7b5, B7b9, Em6). For that reason, the same substitution can be made here as well.

(A7)		ii (F#m7b5)	V (B7b9)	I (Em6)	
A7		(D7)	(D#o7)	(A7)	
1		2		3	4

Bars 2-3 of the following example are based around the same arpeggio scheme used in Examples 5a and 5b. Here, I've added some string-skips to give everything a modern twist, just to show you how it's possible to push the boundaries technically as well as harmonically and still retain a bluesy vibe.

Example 5l

When visualising a quick change, anything you imply in bars 2-3 can also be used in bars 10-11 (and vice versa), because those bars share the same chords.

More ii – V – Is

Because the ii is a suspended version of the V7, we can lead into the D7 of our quick change in bar two by approaching it in the following way:

ii	V	I		
(Em7)	(A7alt)	(D7)	(D#º7)	(A7)
A7				
1		2	3	4

Furthermore, the implied D and D#º7 chords can also be substituted with any of the turnaround cadence variations outlined in Chapter Four (such as D, Dm and D, F7 etc). The following examples follow an implied Em7, A7b9, D, Dm, A7 progression, all played over a static A7 chord.

Example 5m

(Em7)   (A7b9)   (D7)   (Dm)   (A7)

Here's another variation on the same scheme.

Example 5n

(Em7)   (A7b9)   (D7)   (Dm)   (A7)

We can use this same principle to extend the E7 in bar twelve which implies a move from E7sus to E7.

			ii	V
			(Bm7b5)	(E7b9)

E7	D7	A7	E7
9	10	11	12

I
(A7)

A7
1

Example 5o is based on the following arpeggio scheme:

| Bm7b5   E7b9 | A7 |

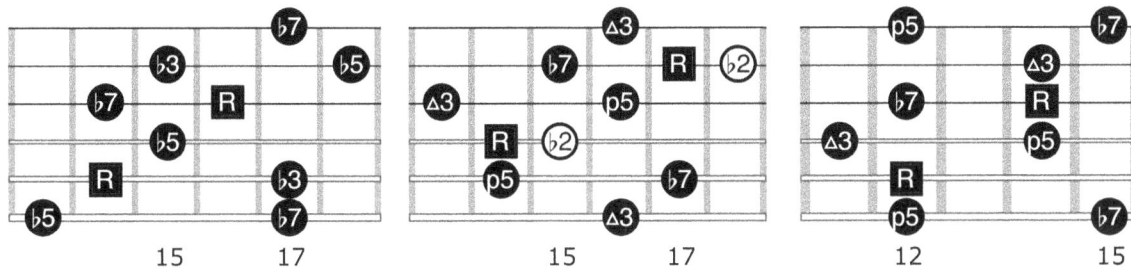

Example 5o

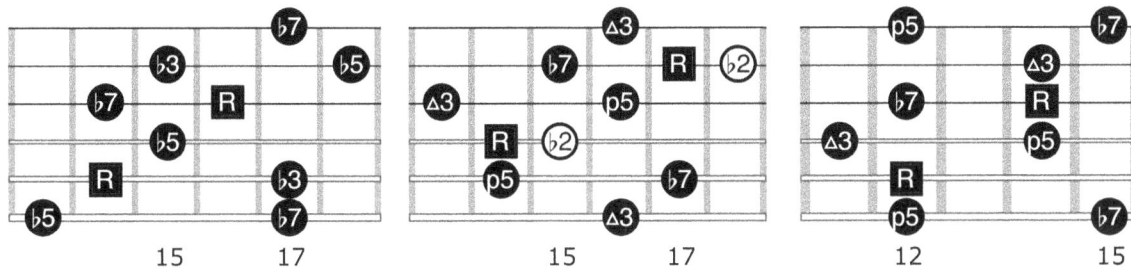

Many of these principles will now be shown in action in the following four demo solos.

Chapter Six: Putting It All Together

The following solos represent a culmination of many of the principles we have studied throughout the book. The goal here is not to produce solos overflowing with theoretical ideas but to find a balance. Simplicity and complexity, space and density, upbeats and downbeats – they all need to work together to create musical interest.

When improvising or composing solos like these, creating balance normally means leaving some ideas out. But don't worry, they can always be used in another chorus or another tune.

Blues Solo #7

Bar One

We begin with a familiar voice: the A Minor Blues scale (1, b3, 4, b5, 5, b7). Our opening phrase starts on the third 1/8th note of the bar and, for thematic continuity, this same rhythmic figure is also repeated in bars two, four and six. There are also a wide range of articulations used in just a few notes – slides, bends, curls – that help to humanise the idea and prevent it from sounding too clinical.

Bar Two

Here, we compress the D7 and D#°7 chords usually implied over bars 5-6 into a shorter space. Any tension this creates is quickly resolved back to the sound of A7.

Bar Three

A quick double-stop slide at the end of this bar adds contrast and balances the texture, breaking up the line so it's not all single-note material.

Bars Four-Five

This section is a good example of theory guiding creativity. By exploring the triads within different scale types, we create a descending sequence of minor triads moving chromatically.

We have:

- Bm (B, D, F#) from E Dorian

- Bbm (Bb, Db, F) from A Superlocrian

- Am (A, C, E) from D Mixolydian

Even though this section is built on a conceptual idea, the presentation remains musical. There are spaces, sustained notes, vibrato, pull-offs and hammer-ons, all within just two bars. The theory gives us structure, but the phrasing brings it to life.

Bar Six

Although you can certainly imply D#°7 in bar six, it doesn't need to start on beat one. D7 will comfortably cover both bars five and six, so the D#°7 can be introduced later in bar six, as demonstrated here. Once again, take note of the expressive phrasing – slides, hammer-ons, and bends – all of which help give the line a vocal, human quality that lifts it beyond just theoretical execution.

Bars Seven-Eight

Now and then, it's satisfying to drop in a pre-prepared line, provided it's set up naturally and doesn't disrupt the musical flow. Here, we hear a classic two-bar Mixolydian-based phrase that lands cleanly on a held note at the 12th fret of the G string. The short four-note tag at the end of bar eight acts as a pick-up into the next idea.

Bars Nine-Ten

As the previous phrase hinted, blues and country often share a similar vocabulary. These two bars explore that crossover with a pedal-steel-style series of double-stop bends. The change in texture is a welcome contrast and breaks up the single-note material.

Bars Eleven-Twelve

We stay with a country-tinged vibe by using staccato, chicken-picking-style articulation over an implied A, A7, D, Dm turnaround cadence. The resolution to A7 in bar twelve feels clean and grounded, and there's even a cheeky reference to E7 to finish.

Blues Solo #7

(Chromatic notes indicated by *)

Blues Solo #8

Bars Zero-One

We begin with a four-note pick-up from A Major Pentatonic (1, 2, 3, 5, 6), followed by a bluesy double-stop targeting chord tones of A7. As usual, this introduces a different texture from single-note lines. A similar effect is used again between bars three and four with an A7 trill.

Bars Two-Three

This section outlines a turnaround cadence often heard in bar eleven (A, A7, D7, D#°7 resolving to A7). Both bars also sit comfortably within the A Half-Whole scale (1, b2, #2/b3, 3, #4/b5, 5, 6, b7).

Bar Four

This phrase features a sweet-sounding variation of A Minor Pentatonic, where the usual b3 (C) is replaced with the 2 (B). Some players, like Stevie Ray Vaughan, might opt for a chromatic trill between A and Bb instead.

Bars Five-Six

This section features a modified two-bar Mixolydian line in CAGED Shape 5, which then shifts into a D#°7 arpeggio.

Note the varied articulation across both bars– slides, pull-offs, and hammer-ons – topped off with a slide into a semitone bend.

Bar Seven

We kick off with a strong, wide-vibrato root note.

What follows is a flurry of quick release bends and repeated double-stop bends in A Minor Pentatonic, echoing the phrasing style of a blues harmonica player.

Bars Nine-Ten

The first six notes of bar nine mirror those in the D Mixolydian line from bar five, reworking the theme in E instead of D. A variation of the same theme follows over the D7 chord in bar ten. This section is built entirely from chord tones, many introduced via chromatic approaches. We begin with a double-chromatic move into G# from both above and below. At the start of bar ten, there's a chromatic descent to D (implying an Eb7), followed by a chromatic approach to F# from below.

Bars Eleven-Twelve

This turnaround uses a familiar structure: a commonly-used scale in bar eleven, resolving to clearly outlined chord tones in bar twelve.

Blues Solo #8

(Chromatic notes indicated by *)

Blues Solo #9

Bars One-Two

The solo begins with a short, implied major ii – V – I (Em7, A7, D7) that immediately flows into a compressed version of the D7, D#°7, A7 cadence usually found in bars 5-7.

Bar Three

We follow with some double-stop bends built from A7 chord tones, offering a break in texture from the single-note lines.

Bar Four

This short blues phrase is brought to life with slides and a semi-harmonic produced by combining thumb flesh and fingernail on the picking hand. This adds a vocal, expressive shimmer to the line.

Bar Five-Seven

Here we imply a full minor ii – V – I (F#m7b5, B7b9, Em6). To keep things expressive and human, the line is filled with articulation – hammer-ons, pull-offs, slides, bends, releases, and vibrato – all balanced with space and rests.

Bar Eight

With experience, instinct takes over. Here, I bent up to a darker sounding b3 over the A7, rather than the sweeter major 3rd, simply because it felt right. Developing a sense of what fits comes from absorbing the feel of blues, soul, and gospel through regular listening.

Bars Nine-Eleven

Like the opening bars, this section features another chain of harmonic movement. In bar nine we imply a major ii – V – I (Bm7, E7, Am7), which then shifts in bar ten as Am7 becomes the ii of another ii – V – I (Am7, D7alt, Gmaj7).

This works because a ii chord can be heard as a suspended version of its related V chord, letting us link Bm7 (E7sus4) to E7alt, then Am7 (D7sus4) to D7alt and so on.

GMaj7 fits comfortably over both D7 and A7, but it's usually best to resolve to A7 in bar eleven, as we do here using chord tones.

Bar Twelve

Silence can say as much as any phrase. Even with all the concepts you've explored, there's no need to fill every space. Let the music breathe when it feels natural to do so. Sometimes, the most expressive thing you can play is nothing at all.

Blues Solo #9
(Chromatic notes indicated by *)

Blues Solo #10

Bars One-Four

We open with a shift through pentatonic flavours that gradually darken the mood. Bar one uses A Major Pentatonic (1, 2, 3, 5, 6), moving into A Minor 6 Pentatonic (1, b3, 4, 5, 6) in bars 2–3, and finally settling into A Minor Pentatonic (1, b3, 4, 5, b7) in bar four.

Bar Six

Following a D Mixolydian idea in bar five, we land on a variation of the D#°7 line from Solo #7; a familiar sound with a fresh contour.

Bars Seven-Eight

Back to A Minor 6 Pentatonic. This time the focus is on a short, rhythmic motif, with aggressive vibrato bringing it to life.

Bar Nine

To keep things balanced, we switch to three-note chord shapes for a bit of textural variety. Note the use of an Eb7 side-slip chord to introduce the D7 at the end of the bar.

Bar Ten

Chord tones are used throughout to imply a D7, D#°7, A7 cadence. This is a compact version of the movement we typically see in bars 5-7.

Bars Eleven-Twelve

We close with an implied A, A7, D, Dm turnaround. In the recorded performance, you'll hear some added harmonic sparkle on selected notes – a semi-harmonic rasp that adds colour without being overbearing. These nuances aren't marked in the transcription, as the level of articulation is yours to choose based on the feel of the moment. Let the notes guide your phrasing.

Blues Solo #10
(Chromatic notes indicated by *)

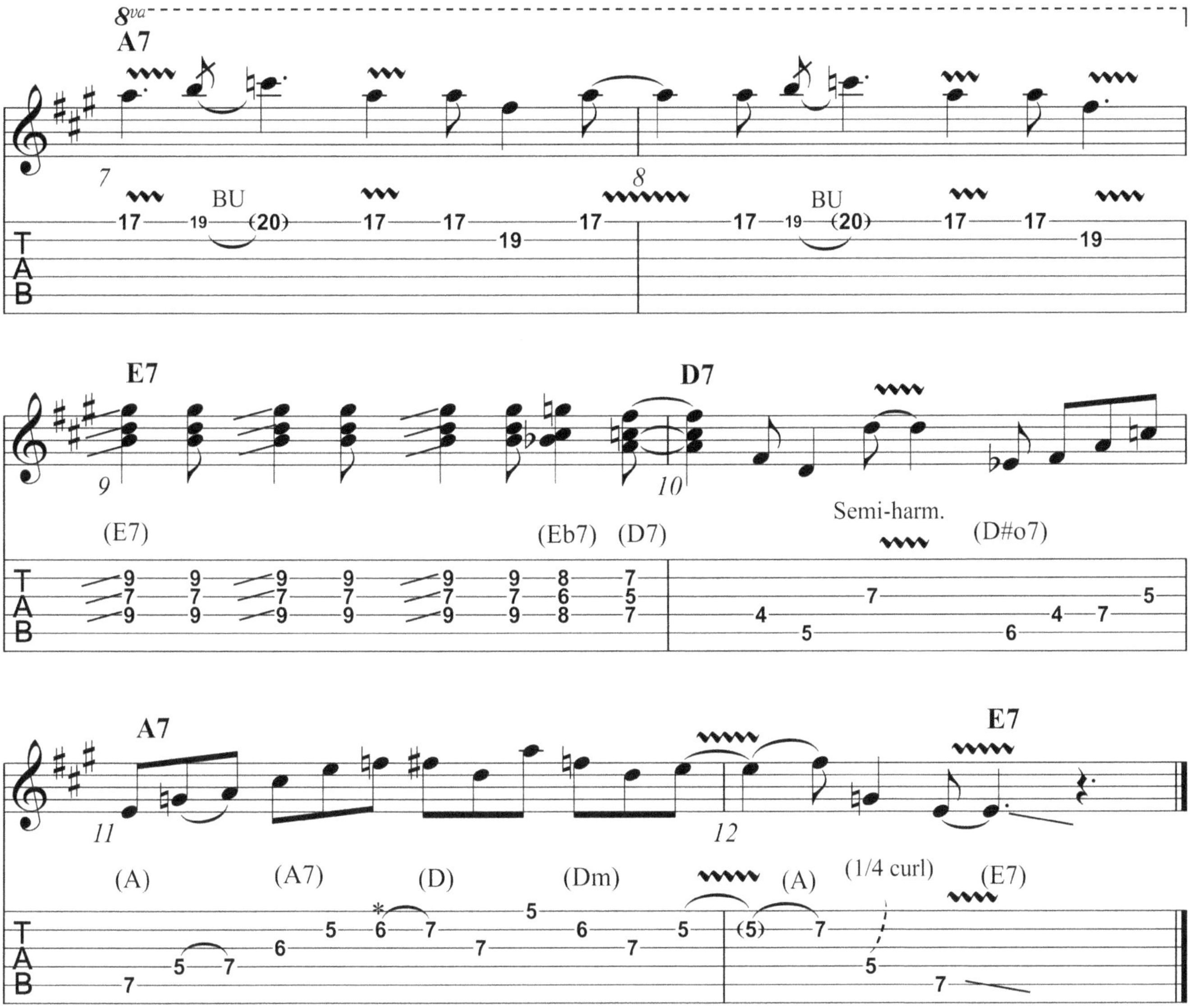

8va
A7
BU
BU
E7
D7
(E7)
(Eb7)
(D7)
Semi-harm.
(D#o7)
A7
E7
(A)
(A7)
(D)
(Dm)
(A)
(1/4 curl)
(E7)

Conclusion

Not every harmonic idea that can be applied to a basic I – IV – V blues progression appears in this book. The ones we have focused on, all built around the concept of a perfect cadence, offer the most accessible entry point. Other approaches, such as those involving Coltrane-style substitutions or motif development through transposition, fall more into the language of modern jazz. While those concepts lie beyond the scope of this book, they are natural next steps for anyone looking to expand their understanding. The core idea here has been to introduce the concept of extended harmony within a simple blues framework, to help create a more sophisticated harmonic sound.

For clarity and consistency, we used the same shuffle backing track throughout. This allowed us to examine each concept within a medium tempo that supports triplet-based eighth-note phrasing. However, this is just one rhythmic context – you also need to explore ideas in duple subdivisions, such as 1/8th and 1/16th notes, and apply these ideas to blues with different grooves, whether funk-inflected, Latin-inspired, or otherwise.

Solid Foundation

As in jazz, it is essential to begin with a simple and reliable foundation. This creates a stable base from which to explore more advanced sounds when the moment calls for them. In blues, the minor pentatonic or minor blues scale serves this role. It remains the safest and most effective choice when other options feel unclear.

Balance

Avoid the temptation to always operate at a high level of complexity. Playing with sophistication does not require constant harmonic density or technical speed. Effective music relies on contrast and nuance. Holding a single expressive note for several bars can carry just as much weight as filling those bars with complex ideas. Let musical context guide your choices.

Theory should not serve as a tool for real-time construction. Instead, treat it as a framework for developing musical ideas that have purpose and direction. With a solid grasp of theory, you can create lines that feel intentional, then reshape them in real time to suit the moment. These ideas should remain flexible, not fixed. Over time, they become tools for genuine expression, grounded in musical logic.

Dynamics

Control over volume and tone is vital to expressive phrasing. Experienced players often adjust their volume between phrases to create contrast and shape. Less experienced players often keep their settings maxed out, which limits their dynamic range. On a slow blues, try setting your volume around 4 and experiment with how the sound evolves as you increase intensity. Switch pick-up positions to explore tonal variation, and consider using your tone knob as part of your phrasing. Eric Clapton's famous "woman tone" came from turning the tone control almost all the way down, and Jeff Beck was known to make tone adjustments constantly between phrases. These tools add depth and personality to your sound.

When you begin to push the envelope and explore new ideas, it is easy to worry about someone saying, "that's not the blues!" but the genre has evolved as different players have introduced new elements over time. Elmore James brought in slide guitar. Billy Gibbons used pinched harmonics. Alvin Lee added a strong country influence. Eric Johnson played fast, fusion-style pentatonic lines. These players each stretched the language while staying rooted in the tradition.

The main thing is to play with the right spirit.

One common feature of the blues is a spluttering, conversational phrasing that defies transcription. At very slow tempos, a player can pour out a flurry of notes in unpredictable rhythms, creating a feel that is almost impossible to write down or reproduce. To develop that kind of expression, you must listen extensively and work at recreating the same flow and energy with the scales and concepts you know.

To keep the material in this book practical and accessible, I chose to present clear, playable ideas at a manageable tempo. Once you absorb the concepts, aim to treat them as tools for fiery, spontaneous expression. That spirit is what gives the blues its raw and lasting appeal for both musicians and listeners.

If this book has inspired you to look deeper into ideas such as altered dominant scales or ii –V – I progressions, and to begin expanding your musical palette in a blues context, then it has achieved its goal.

There is a lot to explore. Each altered dominant scale deserves a book of its own. You will find plenty of material in books and online, although much of it is written for jazz players and presented as streams of eighth notes. It will be your job to reshape that information so that it fits the blues. Some ways to do this include:

• Applying bold articulation through intense vibrato, dramatic slides, and expressive bends

• Placing phrases in unexpected parts of the beat

• Using space deliberately

• Introducing a wide dynamic range

The key remains balance and expression.

Good luck on your musical journey.

Shaun

Summary of Approaches

To wrap things up, here's a summary of key concepts for your reference and further study. Let's begin with a list of useful scales to practice, which can be extracted from the Mixolydian Blues Hybrid scale.

PARENT SCALE	Octatonic Subsets (8-note scales)	Heptatonic Subsets (7-note scales)	Hexatonic Subsets (6-note scales)	Pentatonic Subsets (5-note scales)
9-Note Mixolydian Blues Hybrid: 1, 2, b3, 3, 4, b5, 5, 6, b7	Mixolydian Blues: 1, 2, 3, 4, b5, 5, 6, b7	Mixolydian: 1, 2, 3, 4, 5, 6, b7 Lydian Dominant: 1, 2, 3, #4, 5, 6, b7	Major Blues: 1, 2, b3, 3, 5, 6	Major Pentatonic: 1, 2, 3, 5, 6 Major Pentatonic #2: 1, #2(b3), 3, 5, 6 Indian Pentatonic: 1, 3, 4, 5, b7 Dominant Pentatonic: 1, 2, 3, 5, b7 Dominant Pentatonic #2: 1, #2(b3), 3, 5, b7
	Dorian Blues: 1, 2, b3, 4, b5, 5, 6, b7	Dorian: 1, 2, b3, 4, 5, 6, b7	Minor Blues: 1, b3, 4, b5, 5, b7 Minor 6 Blues: 1, b3, 4, b5, 5, 6	Minor Pentatonic: 1, b3, 4, 5, b7 Minor 6 Pentatonic: 1, b3, 4, 5, 6

Practice extracting each of these subsets from the three CAGED shapes of the Mixolydian Blues Hybrid scale shown in the introduction. Focus on seeing how each one fits within the larger framework so that they become easier to visualise and access when improvising.

Summary of Implied Short Major ii – V – Is

ii	V	I				ii	V
(Em7)	(A7)	(D7)	(D#o7)	(A7)		(Em7)	(A7)
A7							
1		**2**		**3**		**4**	

I		ii	V	I		ii	V
(D7)		(Am7)	(D7)	(Gmaj7)	(A7)	(F#m7)	(B7)
D7				A7			
5		**6**		**7**		**8**	

ii	V	ii	V	I		ii	V
(Bm7)	(E7)	(Am7)	(D7)	(Gmaj7)	(A7)	(Bm7)	(E7)
E7		D7		A7		E7	
9		**10**		**11**		**12**	

I
(A7)
A7
1

Note:

The ii – V in bar eight resolves to E7 (I) in bar nine. The implied Am7 at the start of bar ten is also the I of the previous E7.

Summary of Implied Long Major ii – V – Is (One Bar Per Chord, Instead of Two Beats Per Chord)

ii	V	I		
(Am7)	(D7b9)	(Gmaj7)	(A7)	
D7	(D#o7)	A7		
5	**6**	**7**	**8**	

If the tempo is quick, it is even possible to imply the following, because the tension is not only appropriate but brief.

ii	V	I		
(Bm7)	(E7)	(A7)		
E7	D7	A7	E7	
9	**10**	**11**	**12**	

Although technically incorrect, the implied E7 in bar ten will work because it is the V7 of A7, so any tension created will lead to (and be resolved by) that chord in bar eleven.

Summary of Implied Short Minor ii – V – Is

			ii (C#m7b5) V (F#7b9)
A7			
1	2	3	4

I (Bm7)	ii (F#m7b5) V (B7b9) I (Em6)		
D7	(D7) (D#o7) A7		
5	6	7	8

	ii (F#m7b5) V (B7b9) I (Em6)		ii (Bm7b5) V (E7b9)
E7	D7	A7	E7
9	10	11	12

I (A7)
A7
1

Also:

		ii (C#m7b5) V (F#7b9)	ii (Bm7) V (E7b9)
E7	D7	A7	E7
9	10	11	12

I (A7)
A7
1

Note that the Bm7 in bar twelve is also the I of the previous F#7 chord. Finally, you can also try playing Em7b5 – A7alt in bar four, as Em7b5 is like A7b9sus.

Summary of Implied Long Minor ii – V – Is

ii (F#m7b5)	V (B7b9)	I (Em6)	
D7	(D#o7)	A7	
5	6	7	8

Summary of Implied Turnaround Cadences (Commonly Played in Bar Eleven)

Note that, although A, A7, D, D#°7 is shown in the charts immediately below, it can also be substituted by any of the other harmonically-related variations.

For example:

- A, A7, D, Dm

- A, A7, D, F7

- A, A7, Ab7, G7

- A, C7, B7, Bb7

- A, Eb7, D7, C7

- A, F#7, B7, E7

- A, F#7, Bm7, E7

- C#m7b5, F#7b9, Bm7, E7b9 etc

	(A) (A7) (D) (D#o7)	(A7)	
A7			
1	2	3	4

D7		A7	
5	6	7	8

		(A) (A7) (D) (D#o7)	(A7)
E7	D7	A7	E7
9	10	11	12

Summary of Implied Stretched-Out Turnaround Cadences (Two Beats Per Chord, Instead of Just One)

(A) (A7)	(D) (D#o7)	(A7)	
A7			
1	2	3	4

D7		A7	
5	6	7	8

		(A) (A7)	(D) (D#o7)
E7	D7	A7	E7
9	10	11	12

(A7)
A7
1

And finally, one bar per chord:

		(A)	(A7)
A7			
1	2	3	4

(D)	(D#o7)	(A7)	
D7		A7	
5	6	7	8